"Walter Kaiser has effectively demonstrated that the unifying message of the Messianic promise throughout the Old Testament is recognizable without a need to resort to the New Testament revelation. He illustrates this through helpful exegesis of key Messianic passages within every genre of Old Testament literature. This is an excellent example of the relationship between solid exegesis and biblical theology."

—Gary W. Derickson, Ph.D.
Professor of Biblical Studies and Greek,
Chair of Bible and Theology, Corban University School of Ministry

"As one might expect from a learned veteran of biblical studies, Walter Kaiser's *The Jesus I Know* is rich with insight. Unlike many treatments of this important topic, Kaiser's new book explains Jesus in the light of what Scripture foretells and how Jesus has fulfilled it. This engaging and stimulating book will serve well believers and seekers alike. Highly recommended."

—Craig A. Evans, Ph.D., DHabil
John Bisagno Distinguished Professor of Christian Origins
Houston Christian University

"Once again, Dr. Walter Kaiser, Jr., demonstrates his skill in interpreting the Bible and developing a cogent biblical theology as he explains the central place of the Messiah within the Hebrew Scriptures. Dr. Kaiser's presentation of the Messiah stands in contrast to the belief I encountered with a colleague at an evangelical institution years ago when this fellow faculty member asserted that he did not believe that there were any Messianic prophecies in the Old Testament that related to Jesus, but rather that the authors of the New Testament construed the Old Testament texts to conform to the life of Jesus. This encounter convinced me of the value of pursuing the careful study that Dr. Kaiser has now carefully laid out for his readers in this book.

In *The Jesus I Know (Yeshua the Messiah)*, Kaiser carefully examines the various Messianic texts in the Old Testament, revealing the many ways that Yahweh's Messiah is presented in the biblical text. As well, these point toward the truth that Jesus is the Messiah and Son of God revealed in the New Testament without the need to misconstrue or spiritualize the Old Testament passages. Believers in Jesus as Messiah will be spiritually and intellectually strengthened in the reading of Dr. Kaiser's book."

—H. Wayne House, Th.D., J.D.
Distinguished Research Professor of Theology, Law, and Culture
Faith International University and Seminary

"A thoughtful, and well researched study that provides a renewed appreciation of God's plan and how the biblical authors developed and nuanced Messiah as the center of the Old Testament. Once again, Dr. Kaiser in his winsome and scholarly manner, has produced a wonderful Old Testament Biblical Theology while showing how the Old Testament promises fit into the New Testament and avoiding the pitfalls of altering the Old Testament meaning or promoting some kind of spiritualized double-meaning.

The Jesus I Know (Yeshua the Messiah): The Predicted Messiah and Longed-For King of the World provides grounded theology and nuanced truth that every believer needs in this day of cultural accommodation and theological drift. Thank you, Dr. Kaiser, for being a friend of God and promoter of truth. Your writings have been such a blessing to me in walking with God."

—David Mappes, Ph.D.
Online Professor of Biblical Studies and
Director of Nobility and Knowability Truth Ministries

"Here is the personal testimony of one of this generation's premier Old Testament scholars to the predicted Messiah whose Name is Yeshua (Jesus). He writes with not only a dedication to the text and a deep faith but from a sincere concern for the state of biblical scholarship's recognition of God's promise-plan centered in Messiah. His voice needs to be heard for the sake of preserving both biblical theology and the health of the church."

—Randall Price, Ph.D.
Former Distinguished Research Professor, Liberty University,
Adjunct Professor, Shepherd Theological Seminary,
Veritas International University

THE JESUS I KNOW:

Yeshua The Messiah

The Predicted Messiah and Longed-For King of the World

WALTER C. KAISER, JR.

LAMPION HOUSE PUBLISHING LLC
Navasota, Texas 77868

2023

The Jesus I Know: Yeshua The Messiah
The Predicted Messiah and Longed-For King of the World

Biblical citations are from various versions of the Scripture.

Lampion House Publishing LLC
P.O. Box 1295
Navasota, TX 77868
Website: http://lampionhousepublishing.com/

Printed in the United States of America

ISBN: 979-8-9878598-3-4 (softcover)

First Edition, May 2023

Cover concept by Richard Rose
Cover and interior design/formatting by Vickie Swisher, Studio 20|20

DEDICATION

To
Michael A. Rydelnek
Randall Price
Michael L. Brown:
Special friends and Esteemed Companions
In the work of the Gospel

TABLE OF CONTENTS

INTRODUCTION

In 1975, Gloria and Bill Gaither published a song which found an immediate response in the hearts of joyful believers around the world entitled: "There's Something about that Name." With simple, yet profound witness to the majesty of that name that is above every other name, the song went like this:

> "Jesus, Jesus, Jesus!
> There's just something about that name!
> Master, Savior, Jesus!
> Like the fragrance after the rain.
> Jesus, Jesus, Jesus!
> Let all heaven and earth proclaim.
> Kings and kingdoms will all pass away,
> But there's about that name."

The truth embedded in this song, even though it was more deeply alluded to than always directly affirmed, was that "Jesus the Messiah's" name embodied more than tongue or pen could tell, and there is still something beyond our ability to express the fullness and greatness of his name and person! For while one earthly empire and one mortal ruler and sovereign after another emerged on the world scene to rule for a brief time, the one called Messiah, the Branch, the Redeemer, Savior, and our Sovereign Lord represented someone whose name was beyond all other names and rulers and powers known to any creature in heaven or on the earth!

We have often remarked that the issue of seeing a clear prediction of the Messiah in the Old Testament may well be a defining moment for the evangelical Church and ultimately for the way believers regard Scripture. In fact, the reason why Messianic prophecy is so pivotal entails that Yeshua is the central figure who is expected to arrive on this planet. But if such a prediction cannot be found in the Old

Testament as many revisionists claim, then Old Testament must be re-interpreted by the New Testament so that a Messianic sense can be added to the older text of the Old Testament—the Bible becomes a waxen nose that can be manipulated to say anything we wish it to say. Once manipulated, all authority and all concepts of a divine revelation are totally vacated and removed from being associated with the Biblical text.

This study attempts to select some of the most outstanding and incomparable predications of the great Yeshua, the Messiah and to trace his presence, power, and progress through the history of this world and through the Bible.

CHAPTER 1

THE SEARCH FOR A CENTER TO THE BIBLE'S STORY

One of the areas of Biblical theology where many Bible teachers have some of their strongest disagreements is in what, if anything, constituted the center (German *Mitte*) or controlling message of the Bible as announced in the study of Biblical Theology. In fact, Gerhard Hasel[1] was one who clearly announced the following statement in response to giving an answer to that inquiry:

The question whether the OT [= Old Testament] has something that can be considered its center (German *Mitte*) is of considerable importance for its understanding in doing OT theology. The matter of the center plays an important and at times even decisive role for presentations of OT theology.[2]

Despite this significant acknowledgment of the importance of this issue of the unity of the Bible and the proper understanding of Biblical theology, Gerhart Hasel preferred to speak of a multiplex approach for doing Biblical theology. He asserted limiting the contents of the whole Old Testament to the single idea of a center

1 This essay was originally given in part at the 20th anniversary of the untimely death of my friend Gerhard Hasel (1935–1994).

2 Gerhard Hasel, *Old Testament Theology: Basic Issues in the Current Debate*, 4th ed., Revised and Expanded (Grand Rapids: Eerdmans, 1991), 139.

was an inadequate method of structuring the entirety of Biblical theology. Here is how he put it:

> [the multiplex approach] avoids the pitfalls of structuring a theology of the OT by means of a center, theme, key concept, or focal point but allows for the various motifs, themes, and concepts to emerge in all their variety and richness without elevating any of these longitudinal perspectives into a single structuring concept, whether it be communion, covenant, promise, kingdom of God, or something else. The multiplex approach allows, aside from this, and in the first instance, that the theologies of the various OT books and blocks of writings emerge and stand next to each other in all their variety and richness.[3]

Gerhard did not go on to exactly identify those pitfalls. One could see how a "pitfall" would emerge, however, if it involved importing a concept from *outside* (*ab extra*) the Bible and then using it as the center for all of Scripture. But what if such a "center" presented itself from *within* the body of Scriptural text itself? What if that internal concept showed how cohesive and unified the plan of a single mind and purpose, *viz.*, that that mind and plan came from God himself, and that it embraced the entire multiplexity or plurality of issues into one coordinated whole and developed into a unified plan that embraced the entire corpus of Scripture? Nevertheless, even Gerhard himself could not remain entirely comfortable with his multiplex solution, for on the very next page in his well-written book, he showed some sympathy for the concept of a unifying center. He taught that:

> The final aim of the canonical approach to Old Testament theology is to penetrate through the various theologies of the individual books and groups of writings and the various

3 Hasel, *Old Testament Theology*, 113.

> longitudinal themes to [locate] the dynamic unity that binds all theologies and themes together [into one].[4]

Precisely so! Thus, despite the cautions that Professor Hasel raised, we are never told just how the various theologies of the various Biblical books stood next to each other, nor how they formed one cohesive whole. Indeed, he does recognize that the mere identification of the several longitudinal themes alone is not the totality of the work of the Biblical theologian. But then what would such a quest of the "theology" of the Old Testament look like, as he had conceived a single theology of the Old Testament in its final form?

What is most regrettable, of course, is that Gerhard never got a chance to produce his own complete Biblical theology, to demonstrate just how he would have illustrated and employed such a coordination of the multiplex themes with all their variegated variety to form a single "theology" of the Bible.

Fortunately, however, he wrote an article, which was published posthumously, but even in this article he focused more on some of the cautions he had raised in his earlier works,[5] than in setting forth how a complete Biblical theology, would use this multiplex approach. Nevertheless, he did survey a wide range of suggestions for a center to the theology of the Bible, but he found that the fact that there were so many suggestions proved there was little, or just no real consensus, on any one theme for such a center. Such a quest was beyond the boundaries of good Old Testament scholarship, so he concluded, much to our disappointment. Nevertheless, he did add that if one were to respect the integrity of the contribution of each of the Biblical books, a multiplex approach for a center had to be central to this quest. Gerhard was concerned that any attempt to identify such a center would probably exclude some significant Biblical materials and thus would have resulted in forming a canon within a canon.

---

4 Hasel, *Old Testament Theology*, 114.

5 Gerhard F. Hasel, "Proposals for a Canonical Biblical Theology," *Andrews University Seminary Studies* 34.1 (1996): 23-33.

This, of course, is where we tended to disagree with Gerhard. It would not be necessary for God himself to omit part of his own teaching thus creating a canon within a canon simply by charting a clear course that marked his goal, purpose, and plan in its entirety through all the various Old Testament themes and topics. But before I restate my case for such a center, I will address modifications or criticisms, that must be made for the multiplex approach?

CRITIQUES OF A MULTIPLEX APPROACH

The key question that must be put to those evangelicals, who like Gerhard reject an organizing single center for a Biblical theology (and their number among conservative scholars is quite large indeed), must be this simple question: What then gives the Bible its unity and wholeness to its message? If we contend, as some do, for a discipline called "Biblical Theology" (notice that we speak of it in the singular number:"Biblical Theology"), as opposed to a renaming the discipline as "Biblical Theologies" (the plural number), which few if any have favored. This must imply that there seems to be some way in which all the material is organized around some central principle, theme, purpose, idea, or person, for all 66 books come from a single source, which is our LORD himself! If we assert that there is some type of unity and unifying factor to all the word of God, as most evangelicals eventually do in one way or another, then what will serve as that integrating and unifying plan and structure for the whole canon of Scripture? Will there not need to be some kind of overarching and unifying structure that not only will link the individual books, but also will be one that will link the two testaments as a unified whole? What will show that the Bible is but one book with a single plan or goal and purpose, even though it is spread out over some 1400 years, written in three different languages, with some 40 writers from three continents (Africa, Asia, and Europe) acting under the direction of

God, and who did not collaborate on some kind of continuity for writing their books?

To be more specific, how are we to look at the Old Testament? Do we see a continuity linking the Old Testament promises and fulfillments in the New Testament, or must the old covenant be reinterpreted by the new to be of use for Christians? How shall we read the Old Testament if it is isolated from the New Testament? Should we read the Abrahamic narratives without regard to the Apostle Paul? And if we introduced Paul into the discussion of these patriarchal narratives as a new way of looking at these narratives, would we be misrepresenting the former Biblical narratives and Paul himself as intended by our LORD, and thereby misleading God's people? Did Jesus' coming suddenly change what was represented in the Old Testament stories into a more spiritual, allegorical, or mystical hyper-meaning of the text, that once and for all ended the divine promises offered to the continuously rebellious nation of Israel and now made them written for and about the Church? Did the various books and writers of Scripture have any kind of organizing mind, plan, purpose, and goal within each of them that each writer knew by virtue of revelation from God the Father and that continued God's story to humanity, or were the writers totally on their own to develop what they thought was significant?

As far back as the middle of the twentieth century, H. H. Rowley had already addressed this problem of the wholeness of Scripture in his 1953 book *The Unity of the Bible*:

> There is no automatic spiritual growth of mankind, and the Bible nowhere tells the story of such growth. It records how men of God, acting under a direction which they believed to be [the word] of God, mediated ideas and principles to men. It does not tell how men, by the exercise of their minds, wrested the secret of life and the universe from a reluctant Unknown, but how God laid hold of them and revealed himself through them. If there is any truth in this, then a unity

> of the Bible is to be expected. If God was revealing Himself, then there should be some unity about the revelation, since it was the same Being who was being revealed.[6]

Surely the words of our Lord Jesus to the Samaritan woman must shape the "theological heart of the Bible"[7] when he told her that "salvation is from the Jews" (John 4:23). Even though the discipline of Biblical theology is in the best position to track such a developmental theme through the entire Biblical text, the irony is that in most of the early practitioners of Biblical theology, the emphasis was dominated by the study of the multiple themes of Scripture with presuppositions that were antithetical to the possibility of viewing it as a unified whole.[8] For in the eyes of the greater number of teachers and scholars, the Bible's diversity was too prominent a feature in the Bible to allow for the possibility of a unified whole. That emphasis was carried on from the height of the Biblical Theology Movement in the 1950s and 1970s and even up to our own day in many ways!

Accordingly, few, if any evangelicals who affirm factual inerrancy, want to argue that the Bible does not have something of an overall unity. Few would totally disallow a case for any form of unity or organizational structure to the whole corpus of Scripture! Indeed, would not the fact that disallowing such a supposition against a general or overall unity of the Bible seriously affect the argument for the presence of the divine mind, purpose, and plan of a God for such an order and guiding forethought throughout the whole of Scripture? Surely, God had not left the materials of revelation to be scattered over the pages of Scripture in some haphazardly or disorganized way, despite the reality of a multiplicity of themes and contributing emphases. Instead, Scripture would imitate the same orderliness and purpose that was endemic to the very nature of the

6 H. H. Rowley, *The Unity of the Bible* (Philadelphia: Westminster Press, 1953), 8.

7 A phrase borrowed from Elmer Martens, "Tackling Old Testament Theology," JETS 20 (1977), 123.

8 This is similar to the observation made by Mark R. Saucy, "Israel as a Necessary Theme in Biblical Theology," in *The People, The Land, and the Future of Israel: Israel and the Jewish People in the Plan of God*, ed. Darrell L. Bock and Mitch Glaser (Grand Rapids: Kregel, 2014), 170.

character and person of our LORD himself.

Gerhard's legitimate concerns over whether the declaration of some overarching unity to the Bible would possibly lead to the exclusion of some texts of Scripture, or that it might even develop into forming a canon within a canon, is one that all Biblical scholars should be concerned about, and therefore agree on. Gerhard's concern for retaining the integrity of each Biblical witness is certainly to be applauded. As opposed to some aspects of this concern, however, we would express our concern over those who seem to rush to obtain an incorrect Christological re-interpretation or re-presentation for every Old Testament text by incorrectly using a New Testament as the basis for re-establishing a new or renewed meaning for what it thought the Old Testament had originally meant to say. Each Old Testament text, however, must first be allowed to say what the author, who stood in the counsel of God, obtained, as we must remind ourselves repeatedly, from the Lord who gave us his revelation, rather than our own intrusively and arbitrarily projecting a "Jesus-only" message from every text in the earlier part of the canon. Not every Old Testament text is automatically about Jesus! Some of those texts were meant to reprove, rebuke, and to teach other matters as well!

Others, such as Charles Scobie, agreed with Gerhard Hasel in proposing a Multi-thematic Approach that identifies longitudinal themes, motifs, and concepts.[9] But Scobie likewise failed to show how his organization of this multitrack approach to Scripture resulted in any clear epochs or broadly synchronic structures which showed a progressive and continuing development of any alleged structure or epochs in a plan of God. What was missing was any treatment of the various epochs of Biblical revelation, which showed how the various corpora were diachronically integrated and resulted in clearly identifiable stages in the total and overall promise and

9 Charles H. H. Scobie, *The Ways of Our God: An Approach to Biblical Theology*, (Grand Rapids: Wm. B. Eerdmans Publishing Company, 2003). See Gerhard Hasel. *Old Testament Theology: Basic Issues in the Current Debate*, 4th ed., revised and expanded (Grand Rapids, MI: Eerdmans, 1991), p. 139, and Walter C. Kaiser, Jr., "The Hasel-Kaiser and Evangelical Discussions on the Search for a Center or Mitte to Biblical Theology," Journal of the Adventist Theological Society, 26/2 (2015): 43-53.

propose of God.

From my perspective, the "Promise-plan of God with the Messiah at its heart" shows the best prospect for being the basis for detecting how this salvation from the Jews could become a coherent whole in the discipline of Biblical theology.

HOW THE UNITY OF THE BIBLE IS BUILT AROUND THE PROMISE-PLAN OF GOD

From one end of the Biblical story to the other, Scripture reveals that the Living God uniquely called the world into being simply by the word of his own mouth, and then he called the Jewish people to be his chosen instruments to bring the good news about God's redemption to the world. He purposely located this message of creation and salvation on that part of real-estate that formed a land bridge centered in Israel and the Messiah himself, which existed between the continents of Africa, Europe, and Asia, and as the setting and the place where God would position his people Israel, both in history and in the end day. The choice was solely one that the Living God made—there were no meritorious works or reasons for such a choice of the Jewish people other than his own graciousness and mercy. That divine decision also continues to remain firm, especially despite Israel's apostasy and downright faithless treachery, which might otherwise have signaled an obvious renunciation of one or more of those divine choices. In fact, the nations of the world, which already were benefiting from the divine work of creation, would further benefit from God's choice of Abraham and his line, for Abraham and his descendants were the ones God had designated to be the channel through which the Messiah would come and through whom all the nations would be blessed with the good news of the gospel (Gen 12:3; Gal 3:8).

Paul himself announced that this word given to Abraham in Genesis 12:3 was nothing less the "gospel" itself, God's "good news"

(Gal 3:8). Moreover, Abraham was the first one to be evangelized by his exercise of faith and trust in this coming "Man of Promise," later to be called the Messiah (Gen 15:6; Gal 3:8), when he was promised that one of his own "seed" would embody the substance of God's plan and he himself would be the object of faith in that "good news."

The continuity of this message of creation and the message of the promise of the "Seed" throughout the whole Bible was the real key to the question of unity, for Jesus did not signal a sudden metamorphosis of the text from something old to something new; instead, he claimed that the meaning the text had seminally gone back in the time to the patriarchs and all those who followed them, for it was the identical basis for any and all who would subsequently be justified by faith. Yeshua (= "Jesus") was the One whom the prophets would later point to as the sole object of their faith.

Paul's interpretation of this text was not a new signal for the New Testament community to assign a change, or an alternate meaning to what had been claimed by each writer of the Old Testament. The use of the Old Testament text by the new converts, all the way up to the time of Christ and the apostles, and into our own day, was consistently the same and it matched just how the writers of the older testament had expressed it. The Bible had only one central perception of reality; it represented a single conceptual understanding of the God, in his current and ultimate rule and reign over everything, and in his promise of salvation to all who trusted him; for it was this plan that would embody one continuous hope for all mortals. The promise involved representing a wide variety of a diversity of such plans and doctrines taught, but that did not deter this divine plan from making the main thing the main thing in the plan of God—the promise of God was about his coming as the Messiah who would rule and reign and save all who trusted him.

This is not to say that the current emphasis, or concurrence of those in scholarship, is one where all are agreed on the case for the unity of the Bible; scholarship has probably sided more with the case for the diversity of Scripture, as its leading principle of our day—

even among evangelicals! Gerhard Maier put it this way:

> It is difficult to speak of a "center" of Scripture today, because the rubric "center of Scripture" is often separated from the "unity of Scripture." While the two were closely identified at the time of the Reformation, the Enlightenment disentangled them. Indeed, the "center of Scripture" practically replaced the lost "unity of Scripture."[10]

Nevertheless, it has been my habit in some 60 or more years of teaching Biblical theology to follow the path laid down by Willis J. Beecher in his 1902 Stone lectures at Princeton Seminary, later repeatedly published under the title of *The Prophets and the Promise*. There Beecher defined the promise as:

"God gave a promise to Abraham, and through him to mankind; a promise eternally fulfilled and fulfilling in the history of Israel; and chiefly fulfilled in Jesus Christ, he being that which is principal in the history of Israel."[11]

This promise had ten distinctive features:

1. The Promise-plan of God is found throughout the entire Scripture and not just in selected passages understood in an alternative view known as the promise-fulfillment rubric/scheme. While the Old Testament uses a constellation of words such as "oath," "word," or "pledge," the New Testament settled on using "promise" in its verbal, nominal, and adjectival forms in almost every New Testament book except five of the twenty-seven New Testament books.

2. The Promise-plan of God is regarded in Scripture as a single plan even though it is repeated and unfolded through the centuries with numerous specifications and forms, but

10 Gerhard Maier, *Biblical Hermeneutics*, trans. R. W. Yarbrough (Wheaton, IL: Crossway, 1994), 202.

11 Willis J. Beecher. *The Prophets and the Promise*. (1905, reprint Grand Rapids: Baker: 1975), 178.

always with the same essential core. It became the content of the word given in Eve about her "Seed," the essence of the covenant God cut with Abraham, the word God gave to David about a "house, throne and kingdom," the promise of the Holy Spirit, the inclusion of the Gentiles in the people of God, the promise of Yeshua's death, burial, and sure resurrection, and many more similar doctrines that were all embraced under the single rubric of the "Promise."

3. The New Testament writers consistently equate this single, definite promise (it invariably occurs with the definite article) as the one made with Abraham, when God called him to leave Ur of the Chaldeans.

4. While the New Testament may occasionally speak of "promises," using the plural form of the word "promise," they do not mean thereby to weaken the case for a single, definite promise of God, but only to note that the one definite promise-plan of God has enormous number of doctrines that are justifiably attached to the plan.

5. The New Testament writers view this promise as being composed of many specifications and doctrines that are all embraced in that one single plan.

6. The promise made to Eve, Shem, Abraham, Isaac, Jacob, and David is represented as being partially fulfilled in their time (for example in the exodus), but there was much yet to be realized in the distant future beyond the times of these first recipients.

7. The New Testament writers not only declare that the promise-plan of God can be seen throughout the whole Old Testament, but they adopt the Old Testament phraseology as their own way of speaking of God's revelation to them.

Hence, they talk about the "Seed," the "people of God," the "dynasty of David," the "day of the Lord," etc.

8. Both the Old and New Testaments teach that the promise of God is irrevocable and is operating eternally. Its hallmark was to be "everlasting/eternal."

9. The New Testament makes a strong connection between the promise doctrine and the New Covenant that God would make with "the house of Judah and the house of Israel." Though there never was a covenant specifically given to the Church, the Church participates in that same New Covenant when they by faith are grafted into the one olive tree, which has its roots in the promise God gave to the patriarchs, and in the trunk of the olive tree which is Israel, wherein some of the natural Jewish branches have been lopped off temporarily because of their lack of faith/belief, but all of which can be re-grafted in once again by faith along with the wild branches of the believing Gentiles.

10. The culmination of all these doctrinal specifications is wrapped up in the first and second coming of Jesus Christ. He is the heart and focus of this one definite plan.

SUMMARY[12]

It is especially important to begin, then, as Jesus did with the Samaritan woman: "Salvation is from the Jews." Even more importantly, it is of critical significance that the Gentile Church recognizes that the New Covenant was not made with the structure of the New Testament Church; we repeat, God never made a covenant with the Church.

12 See a fuller description of this argument in Walter C. Kaiser, Jr. *Recovering the Unity of the Bible: One Continuous Story, Plan and Purpose* (Grand Rapids: Zondervan, 2009).

Nor did he place a condition that Israel had to fulfill in the covenant he originally made with Abraham or David in order for them to inherit the blessings of the promise except they must believe; instead, he promised the perpetuity of the contents of his covenant with "the house of Israel and the house of Judah" on into eternity. Thus, disobedient Israelites may be cast outside of his grace, but that does not mean God will forever abandon his promise to Abraham or David. God's plan remains secure and sure for all eternity

CHAPTER 2

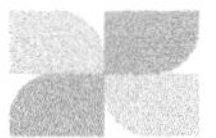

THE MESSIAH AS THE CENTER OF GOD'S STORY

MESSIAH IN THE PROMISE-PLAN OF GOD

Although it may not seem to make much of a difference whether we think of the Tanak's (Old Testament/OT) words about Messiah's person and work as being either scattered "predictions" found throughout the Old Testament or part of a continuing "promise-plan," there was a vast difference in the minds of the Biblical authors in how they present Messiah. For example, a "prediction" is a word foretelling, or a prognosticating, the future. In such a usage, it focuses the reader's or listener's attention only on the two things: the word spoken before the event and the fulfilling event itself, which is proper and legitimate in itself. But when such a usage is attributed to the Scriptures, it fails to capture a third element, which was a key ingredient that captured the hearts and minds of the Old Testament writers: it was the historic means by which God continued to *maintain* his promissory word and to carry it all the way to fulfillment. This is what Willis J. Beecher described in his 1902 Princeton Seminary Stone Lectures called "the Promise." He described it this way:

> [Such a truncated analysis left out] the means employed for that purpose [i.e., the purpose of describing the coming of the Messiah]. The promise and the means and the result are all in mind at once ... If the promise involved a series of results, we might connect any one of the results with the foretelling clause as a fulfilled prediction .... But if we preeminently confined our thought to these items in the fulfilled promise, we should be led to an inadequate and very likely a false idea of the promise and its fulfillment. To understand the predictive element alright we must see it in light of the other elements. Every fulfilled promise is a fulfilled prediction; but it is exceedingly Important to look at it as promise and not as a mere prediction."[13]

In light of this definition, what follows will be a brief outline of the messianic doctrine as set forth in the Bible's own promise-plan and a brief word on its interpretation.

THE MESSIANIC PROMISE-PLAN IN THE TORAH

The messianic doctrine in the Torah may be surveyed under six headings: two in Genesis 1–11, two major ones in the Patriarchal period, and two that dominated the Mosaic period in the rest of the Pentateuch. All six were inter-connected and related seminally to the one grand promise-plan of God, which plan was the backbone of the narrative and theology of the Old Testament.

The first two promises declared that the coming Man of Promise would be from the "Seed," or "Offspring," of the woman in Genesis 3:15, while the second promise announced that no one less than God himself would come and dwell in the midst of the families of

13 Willis Judson Beecher, *The Prophets and the Promise, The Lectures for 1902-1903, The L. P. Stone Foundation in the Princeton Theological Seminary* (New York: Thomas V. Crowell and Company Publishers, 1905), 376.

Shem in Genesis 9:27.

In the second set of promises in the Patriarchal Era, the plan called for Abraham's "Seed" to be the means of blessing all the families of the earth (Gen 12:3). But the plan added more specificity when it named one of Jacob's sons, Judah, as the one who would be given the rule and authority over the nation Israel as well as over all the nations on earth (Gen 49:10).

Two other events stand out during the Mosaic Era of divine revelation. Surprisingly, one comes from a Gentile prophet (the exception that proves the rule that prophecies normally come through Jewish prophets) named Balaam in Numbers 24:17. Balaam raised the promise that the coming Man of Promise would be a victorious king who would crush his enemies and find great success. The second distinctive part of the promise-plan in this period has to be the promise made to Moses that a "prophet," who would be like him, would come in that same plan of God (Deut 18:18).

Even from these earliest and most rudimentary forms, the Torah has anchored this promise-plan with the seminal (i.e., seed) truths that this person who would come in the divine purpose would be known by the titles of "Seed," "Shiloh," "Scepter," "Star," "King," and "Prophet." However, care must be exercised not to take any one of these prophecies or titles in abstraction by itself. Each promise-plan can only be appreciated in their own Biblical context as they contributed to the ongoing announcements and fulfillments of the promise theme. Intertwined in this one plan of God were provisions for a name, a blessing, a land, a gospel, a people, a divine dwelling in the midst of the people, and an affirmation that God himself would be a personal deity to those who called on him by faith. This last feature reminds us of the tri-partite formula of the promise-plan, repeated almost fifty times in both testaments: "I will be your God, you shall be my people, and I will dwell in the midst of you."

While it is difficult to know where to place the book of Job chronologically, even though in genre form it belongs to the wisdom materials in the Tanak, there are very good reasons for placing the events of Job historically and chronologically in the Patriarchal times.[14] Nevertheless, four times in this book a cry goes up to God for someone to act much as the Messiah would in his coming office and ministries.

First of all, in response to Bildad's first speech, Job longs for someone to "arbitrate," or in the older language to be a "daysman," between himself and God (Job 9:33). In a second appeal to heaven, Job longs for a "witness" in heaven who would act as his advocate on high to represent his case (Job 16:19-21). In his third appeal to God, Job pulls out all the stops and declares that he knows his "redeemer" is the one who will raise him up "in the end." Job expects to look on God with his own eyes to see the Living God (Job 19:23-27). In one more final time in this book, the young Elihu, who up to this point has remained silent in the presence of three older friends of Job, called for an "interpreter" who would explain to Job what was going on in his life (Job 33:23-28). This "interpreter" in Job cannot be fulfilled by any angel, a prophet or anyone from the ranks of mortals; This interpreter had to soar beyond the thousands of angels and exceed them in every way in order to redeem Job from the pit of despair and ransom him from all his troubles.

THE MESSIANIC PLAN PRIOR TO AND DURING THE DAVIDIC ERA

The days after Moses started well enough, for Joshua conquered the land in a mighty way, showing God himself was with Joshua as he was with Moses. But that enthusiasm quickly dissipated as a new syncretism engulfed the people and they began to adopt the gods and practices of the Canaanites. In the days of the Judges, Israel entered a dark period of her history.

As the light of revelation progressed toward the close of this

14 For a list of reasons why Job should be placed in the Patriarchal era, see the study by E. Dhorme, *A Commentary on the Book of Job*, trans. Harold Knight (Nashville, TN: Nelson, 1984), xx-xxviii.

dark period of Judges, three major prophecies appeared leading up to David's reign over the nation setting the stage for the new advances in the plan of God.

One prophecy came to Hannah, the mother of the boy Samuel, in 1 Samuel 2:1-10. It represented the fourth stage in royal or kingly themes in messianism. The first promise came to Abraham when he had been promised that "kings will come from [him]" (Gen 17:6, 16), as God reaffirmed the same to Jacob, "kings will come from your body" (Gen 35:11). In the second stage, the symbols of rule and authority (the "scepter" and "ruler's staff") were given to Judah (Gen 49:10), through which royal authority would claim the "obedience of [all] nations." The third stage depicted this coming king in the Messianic line crushing his enemies in the Balaam prophecies about a "star [coming] ... out of Jacob" and a "scepter ... out of Israel" (Num 24:17). In 1 Samuel 2:10 the fourth stage had been reached: Messiah would be the exalted King and Judge over all the earth.

There was more to messianism than its earthly royal or kingly theme; a priestly messianism could be seen in germ form as far back as Exodus 19:6, where the whole nation was called to be "a kingdom of priests." But this aspect was further clarified by an unnamed prophet who was sent to the priest Eli in 1 Samuel 2:35-36 to say that God would raise up "a faithful priest who would do according to what was in [God's] heart and mind." But who was this "faithful priest"? The Hebrew word for "faithful," *ne'eman,* is the same root used of David's house in 2 Samuel 7:16, a "house and .... Kingdom [which] <u>will</u> <u>endure</u> forever" (which 1 Sam 25:28 repeats as "a <u>lasting</u> dynasty"). The identity of the faithful priest mentioned here is to be understood as a collective expression, embracing all priests whom God raised up for altar duty and who collectively culminate in Messiah, the final one and only real "faithful priest."

At the heart of the five promise-peaks in this era is 2 Samuel 7, where the prophet Nathan predicted King David: (1) Messiah would come from his flesh and seed, (2) Messiah would be David's climactic heir, (3) David's son and the Messiah would be God's own son, (4) Messiah would have a kingdom, a rule, and a reign that would never end, and (5) Messiah would surely come one day in the future.[15]

Regarding this key promise made to David, two Psalms echo this important and central point in the promise-plan of God: Psalm 89 and Psalm 132. The messianic part of Psalm 89 is found in verses 19-37. It repeats some twelve promises made by the prophet Nathan to David, despite the way the Psalm ends on the mournful note that David's throne and kingdom were at that time in a dilapidated condition. But the taunts of the nations will be answered as God rises once again to vindicate his plan. In Psalm 132, three symbols describe Messiah: "a horn," "a lamp" (already seen in 2 Sam 21:7; 1 Kgs 11:36), and "a crown." With such high accolades, there is little doubt that the anointed one is not just David and his line of kings, but the Messiah himself.

THE MESSIAH CELEBRATED IN ELEVEN PSALMS

J. Barton Payne declared that the single largest block of predictive material on the Messiah in the Old Testament was to be found in the Psalms.[16] He counted some 101 verses directly predicting the Messiah in thirteen different Psalms. Since we have already treated two of the Psalms in the Davidic section (Pss 89, 132), we have time and space to only list the eleven additional Psalms here.

Psalms 2 and 110 address Messiah as a conqueror and enthroned ruler. Another Psalm, 118, describes Messiah as a rejected stone by Israel. Two other Psalms, 69 and 109, see Messiah as betrayed. But two of the most important of this group, Psalms 22 and 16, deal with his dying and rising again in resurrected form. Add to this Psalms 40

15 See, Walter C. Kaiser, Jr., "Messiah In the Promise Plan of God," Part 1, Torah Class, https://torahclass.com/messiah-in-the-promise-plan-of-god-part-1-by-walter-c-kaiser-jr/.

16 J. Barton Payne. *Encyclopedia of Biblical Prophecy* (New York: Harper and Row, 1973), 257.

and 45, where Messiah is addressed as a planner and a groom, while Psalms 68 and 72 declare Messiah to be the triumphant king.

THE MESSIAH PREDICTED IN THE LATTER PROPHETS

One would have thought that the promise-plan of Messiah would have ended when the predictions made to Eve, Shem, Abraham, Isaac, Jacob and David were fulfilled. Surprisingly enough, this was only the beginning, for now these same promises begin to proliferate and blossom way beyond anything anyone could have imagined once we come to the sixteen writing "Latter Prophets." These prophets exhibit thirty-nine direct predictions concerning the Messiah. Yet what they wrote was no mere day-dreaming of a better day and time of blessing for all concerned; instead what God was going to do through his coming Messiah became the basis for repentance and a real change of heart in the present. This is because the promise doctrine had a two-fold character: it was a standing prediction of what God would do in the future, as well as a doctrine which men and women could live by in that era.

The Ninth Century: Messiah as a Teacher

The prophet Joel is probably set in the 800s BC, though this cannot be stated with certainty. In Joel 2:23 he speaks of God sending his Messiah as a "The Teacher" (Hebrew, *hammoreh*). Some want to render this Hebrew word as "rain," but the Hebrew for that would be *yoreh*, which appears later in this verse. Indeed, the blessing of God in sending his Messiah as "the Teacher" is depicted in terms of the coming of rain and fruitfulness on the land after a time of locusts invasions and a famine. Thus, the coming of God's Teacher signals the autumn and spring rain in their seasons to bring Messianic blessing of the covenant.

The Eighth Century Non-Isaianic Prophecies

There are four prophecies during this period from three writing prophets: Hosea 3:4-5; Amos 9:11-15; Micah 2:12-13; and Micah 5:1-4. While Joel focused on Messiah as Teacher, Hosea emphasized his kingship, throne, dynasty and kingdom. He acknowledged that even though Israel would be a long time without sacrifices, an ephod, or the services of a king, yet when Israel returned and sought the Lord, the new David would come as king with his blessings in the last days.

Amos also acknowledged that the mighty house of David was at that time in a dilapidated state, but God would once more raise it up in that latter day as he unified the divided nation, rebuild the dynasty of David and brought what had to be the new or second David back to the rule and reign of a kingdom that would extend over all the earth. Amos 9:11-15 states God would do this so that both the remnant of Israel and all in the nations who were owned by the Lord, and had his name called over them, might be under Messiah's dominion.

In this same eighth century BC, the prophet Micah saw Messiah as the "Breaker" (Mic 2:12-13,) who would open up the gate so that those who had been pent up could now be released and enjoy God's salvation. Indeed, Micah 5:1-4 told us exactly where Messiah was to be born: in Bethlehem. And Messiah would rule as the ancient plan finally takes its final shape.

The Eighth Century Prophecies of Isaiah

Few prophets are as detailed in their predictions about the coming Messiah as the prophet Isaiah. He, under the inspiration of God, contributed fourteen parts to the promise-plan. There is only time to briefly list some of the magnificent prophecies that Isaiah set forth in his writing.

Isaiah 4:2 emphasizes that Messiah will be known as the "Branch of the LORD," surely referring to Messiah's divinity. This coming

Man of Promise would also be born of a virgin (Isa 7:14) and carry a most awesome set of names and titles: "Wonderful Counselor, Almighty God, Everlasting Father, Prince of Peace" (Isa 9:1-7). In Isaiah 11:1-16 Messiah's reign is described, while Isaiah 24:21-25 treats Messiah's universal triumph and his defeat of Satan when he was released after being bound in prison "many days." Other Isaianic texts treating the Messianic promise are 28:16; 30:19-26; 42:1-7; 49:1-6; 50:4-9; 52:13-53:12; 55:3-5; 61:1-3; and 63:1-6.

Seventh Century Prophecies of Jeremiah

Just as Isaiah used the "Branch" to talk about Messiah, so also did the prophet Jeremiah. In 23:5-6 he used this same symbol for the Messiah, who according to Isaiah would also come from the line of David. Later, in Jeremiah's Book of Comfort (Jer 30–33), the prophet makes it clear once again that God would raise up "David their king" "in that day" (Jer 30:8-9), and that king would also be a priest (Jer 23:21c). The prediction of Jeremiah 23:5-6 is essentially repeated in Jeremiah 33:14-26.

Sixth Century Prophecies of Ezekiel and Daniel

Ezekiel, the younger contemporary of Jeremiah likewise ministered from the Babylonian exile. In his view, Messiah would grow up as a "tender sprig" (Ezek 17:22-24), yet he would rule as the One "to whom [the throne of David] rightfully belonged" (Ezek 21:25-27)—a filling out of the meaning of the cryptic word "Shiloh" in Genesis 49. Ezekiel also set forth Messiah as the "Good Shepherd" in Ezekiel 34:23-31. But Ezekiel's greatest prophecy was in 37:15-28, where Messiah was seen as the great unifier of the divided kingdom of Israel. He would once again join the two houses of Ephraim (the ten northern tribes) and Judah (the two southern tribes) into one nation under his leadership.

Daniel, just a like Ezekiel, was carried off into captivity in Babylon with his three friends Meshach, Shadrach, and Abednego. For Daniel, Messiah came as the "Son of Man" in Daniel 7:13-14 to receive the kingdom and authority from God the Father. Messiah was the "Anointed One" who would come in Daniel 9:24-27 as "the Ruler," and the one who would defeat the "little horn" that represented the evil one and all his forces.

Fifth Century Post Exilic Prophets

There are eleven major Messianic prophecies in this final time-period where the plan of God was unleashed: two were from the prophet Haggai, seven were from the prophet Zechariah, and a final two came from the prophet Malachi.

Haggai 2:6-9 saw Messiah as "the Desire of all the Nations." He also reported that Messiah was the "Signet Ring" (Hag 2:21-23), which was the God-ordained emblem of the office and authority of the Davidic kingship.

But in this post-exilic era, few were more specific and graphic in detailing the life and ministry of Messiah than the prophet Zechariah. He again included the work of a High Priest in the ministry of Messiah (Zech 3:8-10). This Messiah would be a Priest-King over all the nations on earth in that final day (Zech 6:9-15). Messiah's kingly aspect would be noted more definitely in Zechariah 9:9 as he would ride into Jerusalem on a donkey. This prophet also gave Messiah four titles in Zechariah 10:4. He, as the "cornerstone," would be the foundation and unifier of those who belonged to him by right of redemption. Secondly, he would be the "tent peg" or "nail," where everything would be secured in the household of faith. Thirdly, he would be the "Battle-bow," a symbol of strength for his military conquests as he secured the kingdom. Finally, Messiah would the "taskmaster," the absolute Ruler on whom all sovereignty rested. Zechariah 11:4-14 noted that Messiah would be rejected by his own people Israel and he would be "pierced" by them (Zech 12:10), but those setbacks would not last, nor would the smiting of Messiah as noted in Zechariah 13:7. Messiah would emerge triumphant over all these adversities and he would rule from Jerusalem as King of kings and Lord of lords.

The prophet Malachi described Messiah as the "Messenger of the Covenant" (Mal 3:1), who would purify the Levites when he came, but he would also judge all unrighteousness. The final title given to Messiah in the Tanak is the "Sun of Righteousness" in Malachi 4:2. Messiah would come with healing in his wings like the bursting forth of the sun at sunrise.

THE MESSIAH IN MODERN INTERPRETATIONAL SCHEMES

Given this plethora of references to the Messiah in the Tanak, even on a selective basis, the modern conclusion of Joachim Becker is easily refuted as he summarized his study of Messiah: "there is not such a thing as messianic expectation until the last two centuries BC."[17] But even Becker could not support his own conclusion, for he wondered how such a conclusion could be reconciled with one of the most central affirmations of the New Testament, which with "unprecedented frequency, intensity, and unanimity [insisted that] Christ was proclaimed in advance in the Old Testament."[18] Becker evaded is own dilemma by appealing to the method of exegesis in late Judaism, namely *Pesher* exegesis,. *Pesher* exegesis denied that there was a historic meaning to the Messianic references in the Old Testament, but the text could be interpreted and applied outside its historical, contextual setting in order to make the Messianic texts serve a new Christian point of view.

Such bold statements by Becker entail why we are displeased with those in our circles who assert a "Double Meaning" of prophecy. According to this view, there is a distinction to be drawn between what the prophet had intended as they wrote from their historical limited perspectives and what God the Holy Spirit meant by the

17 Joachim Becker, *Messianic Expectations in the Old Testament*, trans. David E. Green (Philadelphia: Fortress, 1980), 93.

18 Becker, *Messianic Expectations*, 93.

same utterance. But as Milton Terry warned, "If Scripture has more than one meaning, it has no meaning at all."[19]

The Promise-Plan view avoids both extremes set forth by a *Pesher* type exegesis and a Double Meaning type exegesis. There is a single, unified, continuing, purpose and plan that is organically related as the seminal germ in a seed is related by the final fully developed plant and all the stages of growth found in between the two ends of this process. It is this plan and this method of interpretation that I commend to the body of Christ and to all believers everywhere.[20]

SUMMARY

This chapter overviews the promise-plan of God demonstrating that Messiah is indeed the center of God's story. The promise of the seed (offspring) of the woman erupts from Genesis 3:15 and is developed through a series of Scriptures which are all organically connected from the Patriarchs to Abraham and to Israel. The book of Job, most likely portraying patriarchal events, also contributes to the Genesis 3:15 seed promise. The seed-promise is significantly developed through the Balaam oracles (Numb 24:17), the end of the period of Judges, the Davidic reign (2 Samuel 7) and the Psalter, notably Psalm 2; 22; 110; 89; 132). Each era of the Prophets emphasizes and portrays the promise-plan of God. Messiah will come from a virgin (Isaiah 7) and his work is described as a Teacher, a Branch, a Good Shepherd, the Son of Man, and a Signet ring. Zechariah emphases that Messiah will be a cornerstone while Malachi states Messiah will be a Messengers of the Covenant. Each aspect of the promised Messiah is organically connected to the other to show unity to God's promise-pan.

19 Milton Terry, *Biblical Hermeneutics* (New York: Eaton and Mains, 1890), 384.

20 The basic thrust of this lecture can be seen in more detail in Walter C. Kaiser, Jr., *The Messiah in the Old Testament* (Grand Rapids: Zondervan, 1995) and my other book entitled *The Promise-Plan of God* (Grand Rapids: Zondervan, 2008).

CHAPTER 3

THE MESSIAH AS THE FOURFOLD "BRANCH"

The promises on the first and second coming of Messiah form the heart of the promise-plan of God in the Old Testament. Some, of course, are not convinced that the Tanak (Old Testament/OT) actually presents two comings of the Messiah. The conventional wisdom of many Jewish authors through the centuries has been that the Tanak only mentions the arrival of the Messiah when there is a time of peace (*shalom*), such as is mentioned in Zechariah 9:9-13. However, in that very same context (Zech 12:10), mention is made of the fact that "they will look on me (the Almighty), the one they have pierced, and they will mourn for him as one mourns for an only child..."

In a televised debate I had some years ago[21] with Rabbi Dr. Pinchas Lapide, he too declared that Christians emphasized two comings of the Messiah, whereas Jewish people only looked for Messiah to come once and only in a time of peace, so it was not time yet for the Messiah to appear. I responded, nevertheless, that the Tanak did feature two comings of Messiah in the very Zechariah context we were discussing. If Israel will look on the Almighty in Zechariah 12:10, the one who was pierced, I noted: "How and when did he get pierced?" The Rabbi said he did not know; I answered: "I have

21 On the John Ankerberg Show. When?

an idea when he was pierced; when the Messiah came the first time."

Messiah is heralded with several titles in the Old Testament. For example, the prophet Jeremiah warned the people of his day: "they have forsaken me, the Spring of Living Water" (Jer 2:13). Could this be what Jesus was referring to in John 4:14? "The water I give him will become in him a spring of water welling up into eternal life." Or take another title: "King." Jeremiah again taught: "They will serve the LORD their God and David their king, whom I will raise up to them." What about one more title: "Redeemer?" Jeremiah 50:34 announced: "Their Redeemer is strong: the LORD Almighty is his name."

But one of the most dramatic names for Messiah is the name "Branch" (Hebrew, *tsemach*). It is under this title that four presentations of Messiah are given, which the early Church Fathers likened to the four Gospels of Matthew, Mark, Luke and John. The four titles of "Branch" were:

The Messiah, the Kingly Branch: Jeremiah 23:5-6; parallel to Matthew.

> "The days are coming, declares the LORD, when I will raise up to David a righteous Branch, a king who will reign wisely..."

The Messiah, the Servant: Zechariah 3:8; parallel to Mark.

> "Listen, O high priest Joshua and your associates seated before you, who are men symbolic of things to come: I am going to bring my Servant, the Branch.... And I will remove the sin of this land in a single day."

The Messiah, the Man: Zechariah 6:12; parallel to Luke.

> "Tell him this is what the LORD Almighty says: `Here is the man whose name is the Branch, and he will branch out from his place and build the temple of the LORD."

The Messiah, the Divine One: Isaiah 4:2; parallel to John.

> "In that day the Branch of the LORD will be beautiful and glorious, and the fruit of the land will be the pride and glory of the survivors in Israel."

Each of these four promises about the Branch arose in the context of great despair and hopelessness over the immediate situations in which the nation found itself at that time. These four portraits exhibit four different aspects of Messiah. Each aspect entails a different preaching emphases- just as a gifted painter would not include every aspect of a person in a single portrait, but would paint four distinct portraits to emphasize each aspect of a person, so we will go to each of the four texts mentioned above to give a more rounded and fuller picture of Messiah for those to whom we will preach. These four texts and the four Gospels each emphasize a distinctive aspect of the Messiah that are all part of the total picture.

TEXTS: JEREMIAH 23: 5-6; ZECHARIAH 3:8; ZECHARIAH 6:12-13; AND ISAIAH 4:2

Title: "Four Aspects of Messiah's Character"[22]

Homiletical Keyword and Interrogative "aspects of Messiah: What are the four essential aspects of Messiah's character taught in the Old Testament)?

Outline:

- ***I. Messiah the Kingly Branch of David – Jeremiah 23:5-6***
- ***II. Messiah the Servant Branch – Zechariah 3:8***
- ***III. Messiah, the Man, the Branch – Zechariah 6:12-13***

22 For the basic ideas and some of the content of this these sections, I am beholden to the marvelous chapter III by David Baron in *Rays of Messiah's Glory: Christ in the Old Testament* (Grand Rapids: Zondervan reprint of 1886: n.d.), 72 –128. It is a classic chapter on this topic.

IV. Messiah, the Divine One, the Branch – Isaiah 4:2

I. Messiah, the Kingly Branch of David – Jeremiah 23:5-6

Messiah is introduced as the Son of David because he is the "King" who will rule and reign the world from Mount Zion in Jerusalem and do so gloriously (Isa 24:23). God made an ancient covenant with David that one of his descendants would sit on that very throne of David as an everlasting and an eternal covenant (2 Sam 23:5). Rather than this being a figurative expression, it pointed to the fact that Jeshua (Jesus) would literally reign in Zion over the Jewish nation and the nations of the world.

When Yeshua was born in Bethlehem, the angel Gabriel announced this child: "He will be great and will be called the Son of the Most High. The Lord God will give him the throne of his father David, and he will reign over the house of Jacob forever; his kingdom will never end" (Luke 1:32-33). There is some debate whether this is the same throne on which Jesus now sits "at the right hand of the Father," or whether there is also a future throne of David; one throne in heaven at the right hand of the Father and another earthly thrown in Zion for future occupancy of the final one in the line of David, Yeshua. Classic dispensationalists assert there is only earthly davidic throne whereas Progressive Dispensationalists argue that Jesus is currently on the davidic throne in heaven and presently ruling. The only passage that would seem to indicate that Yeshua is now exalted on the throne of David is Acts 2:29-36. There Peter preached that since David was a "prophet," he "knew that God had promised him on oath that he would place (Greek, *kathisai*) one of his descendants on his throne." The question for this text, however, is this: is Christ now in possession of that throne for his future ruling session though currently interceding and ruling according to his priestly role, or is he presently (note the Greek tense) seated and ruling on that throne exercising Davidic prerogatives? The present text could fit both meanings. No one doubts that Jesus is the King who would succeed

David, nor that he is now seated on a throne; the thornier question is: is Christ seated on the Father's throne until he occupies his own Davidic throne in the future, as Revelation 3:21 suggests ("To him who overcomes, I will give the right to sit with me on my throne, just as I overcame and sat down with my Father on his throne"), or is Messiah already on David's throne? Some add, for good measure, Hebrews 10:12-13. "But when this priest had offered for all time one sacrifice for sins, he sat down at the right hand of God. Since that time he waits for his enemies to be made his footstool..." Christ now occupies a priestly throne at the right hand of God, but it is not his permanent seat, but only one given to him until his enemies are defeated and he appears a second time to sit on the throne of David and rule the earth.

In our Lord's parable of the nobleman who went into a far-off country "to receive for himself a kingdom and to return" (Luke 19:12-27), many point to the fact that Messiah commences his kingdom after he returns to earth and not before.

Regardless of which view is adopted (presently on the throne of David or seated at the right hand of the Father until he returns to occupy his throne in Zion), it is clear that when he does return he will rule over Israel and the nations from Mount Zion, seated on David's throne. At the present time, Israel is living without a king or prince as taught Hosea 3:4, but that condition will cease when Messiah returns: "Afterward the Israelites will return and seek the LORD their God and David their king. They will come trembling to the LORD and to his blessings in the last days" (Hos 3:5).

In that future day when Messiah returns, Israel will finally recognize Christ as the One "whose right it is to reign" (Ezek 21:27). Whereas they cried at his death, "crucify him, crucify him," now they will shout: "Hosanna! Blessed is He who comes in the name of the LORD" (Ps 118:26). He will be recognized as the One they had waited for (Isa 25:9), even though he had been labeled in the past as "the Stone the builders rejected."

II. Messiah the Servant, the Branch – Zechariah 3:8

A second aspect appears in the prophet Zechariah. In Zechariah 3:8 we have Joshua the High Priest standing before the Lord at the altar in filthy garments defiled and besotted by sin, with Satan ready at hand to prosecute and accuse Joshua and Israel for her sinfulness. In a strange way, Satan wants to point out Israel's sin and to instruct God that that nation is not worthy of being forgiven, since God is too holy to have such sinners in his presence! The High Priest, Joshua represented Jerusalem and the land of promise, while Satan sought only Israel's destruction on account of her sinful defilement; all the while, Satan is the very essence of sinful, defilement. Nevertheless, Satan was correct; Israel was defiled by her sin. But what Satan needed to hear in God's rebuke is what the people in Zechariah's day as well today need to hear: "The LORD said to Satan, `The LORD rebuke you, Satan! The LORD who has chosen Jerusalem, rebuke you! Is not this man a burning stick snatched from the fire?'" (Zech 3:2) referring to both Joshua the high priest and to Israel who Joshua was representing; Israel would be pulled out of the flames as well.

Satan is forever silenced by the rebuke of God. But if asked how God could still be "just" and "righteous" in taking away the sin of nation represented as the filthy garments the High Priest Joshua was wearing, the reply is ready at hand in this text: "Behold, my servant the Branch I am going to bring forth" (Zech 3:8). In this way God can be both "the Just and the Justifier" of all those chosen by him. From the service of the Branch, God's justice and his grace can outshine any filth that has stained the priestly representative of the people.

Not all have agreed with this interpretation of the Branch-Servant. For example, Kimchi and Rashi saw this servant to be Zerubbabel. Yet as they claimed this to be the correct interpretation, they also acknowledged that the older view among the Jewish people was that it was the Messiah. They fail to justify why they departed from the Messianic interpretation. Indeed, the Targum Yonathan introduced Messiah by name in this very text of Zechariah 3:8. Strangely enough, Kimchi acknowledged that the title "Branch" meant Messiah in Isaiah 4:2 and Jeremiah 23:6. Moreover, the words of Zechariah 3:8 do not agree with Zerubbabel's circumstances, for the prophet Zechariah said, "I will bring forth my Servant the Branch." However, in this passage, Zerubbabel already was on the scene and was a prince among them, as Abarbanel, a most antagonistic opponent of Christianity, so forthrightly pointed out to these erring Rabbis. Abarbanel went on to note that nothing further happened to Zerubbabel after this prophecy, for he received no royal status, no royal kingdom, or any further dignity than he already possessed at the time of the writing of this prophecy.

In the servant role, Messiah, as the "Son of Man did not come to be served, but to serve, and to give his life as a ransom for many" (Mark 10:45). He had to pay for us by his death as a substitute for the ransom none of us could give. We sinners cannot atone for our own sins since we are sinful and hence incapable of doing so. Even when we have done all we can, we are still unworthy of the saving grace of God. Grace only comes because of God's mercy to ransom each of us who believe.

III. Messiah, the Man Whose Name is Branch – Zechariah 6:12-13

The third aspect of Messiah's character is that he is just as fully human as he is divine. Once again Rashi, Aben Ezra, and Kimchi argued that "the Man the Branch" was Zerubbabel, the governor of Judah, but they departed from the received interpretation of the earlier Jewish interpreters as is clear from the Targum Yonathan, where he paraphrased verse 12 as, "Behold the Man; Messiah is His Name." Again Abarbanel decisively refuted this trio of Jewish commentators even though he did not share any reasons to promote one position or the other.

Messiah's birth surely demonstrated that he was fully human. Some will immediately object, however, that if Yeshua were truly a human man, then he must be born in the same manner as every other man. But does the fact that he had a miraculous birth from a Jewish virgin (Isa 7:14; 9:6) detract his common humanity with us.

But this objection proves too much, for if that argument stands, then it would force us to deny the true humanity of the first man and all who descended from him. Adam also had a most unusual birth, for he was born not by the same process as other mortals are born. This argument would in effect deny the real humanity of the man Adam from whom all other men have sprung! Therefore, few will want to argue in this manner since the quality or definition of manhood does not depend on the manner in which an individual came into existence. It rests, instead, on certain qualities that make up humanity.

The case for Yeshua's humanity can also be made from the Angel of the Lord appearances in the Tanak (e.g. in Gen 18:2, 13; Josh 5:14-15; Judg 6:11, 12-22). The fact that this "Angel of the LORD" appeared in pre-incarnate human form prepared us for Christ who in the fullness of time came as a real human man—only this time he would remain permanently in that human form. The angels taught the men of Galilee as they watched Jesus ascend into heaven, "This same Jesus, who has been taken away from you into heaven, will come back in the same way you have seen him go up into heaven" (Acts 1:11). Or, in 1 Timothy 2:5 Paul taught, "there is one God and one mediator between God and men, the man [his permanent form] Christ Jesus."

Once, when I was teaching an African-American 8-10 year old boys Sunday School class, Freddy asked me, "What will God look like when we see him?" For the moment I was stunned by the question and quickly ran through my mind the various creedal formations. Suddenly the Holy Spirit brought to my mind John 14:8-14, where Philip asked Jesus the same question: "Show us the Father and we will be satisfied." Yeshua responded to Philip, "Have I been so long a time with you and yet have you not known me? He that has seen me has seen the Father" (AV). So I told Freddy, "God will look like Jesus, Freddy." He too, like Philip in Jesus' day, was satisfied.

Messiah will "branch up from under him" (literal rendering of Zech 6:12), i.e., he will grow up and he will build the temple. While there are several ways the building of the temple could be understood, Ezekiel does foretell and describe in great detail a temple that would be built at the time of the second advent (Ezek 40–44). No longer would this temple have inscribed over its gates, "No stranger shall enter into it." Instead, it will summon: "Come, let us go up to the mountain of the LORD and to the house of Jacob, and he will teach us his ways and we will walk in his paths, for the law will go forth from Zion and the word of the LORD from Jerusalem" (Isa 4: 2-4). Surely, this one born of the virgin Mary, whom lived and walked among us in our kind of world, is truly man.

IV. Messiah, the Branch of the LORD – Isaiah 4:2

The fourth and final aspect of Messiah's character is his divinity. The prophet Isaiah has chosen to speak of this aspect of his character because he wants to emphasize that Israel will be "purged" of their sin and "washed" from the stain and guilt of their iniquity. But who can forgive sins but God only? Therefore, the aspect of his divinity had to be brought forth in this connection. It will take no one other than God to forgive and cleanse this old sinful world of the guilt on each mortal's heart.

In this instance, Rashi said that the "Branch of the LORD" pointed to the righteous remnant in Israel, but Kimchi said this Branch of the LORD was "Messiah ben David, as it is written, 'Behold I will raise unto David a righteous Branch.'" Yonathan paraphrased this text in his Targum the "Branch of the LORD" as "the Messiah of God." Who else could it be if sin was to be effectively treated?

When Israel's sin is purged and removed, once again Israel will be remarried to the Lord. Just as God is presented as remarrying Israel in Isaiah 62:5 "as a young man marries a virgin" and "as a bridegroom rejoices over his bride," so Isaiah 4:5d mentions the Hebrew **Huppah**, "beyond all this glory shall be the marriage canopy." The deliverance of the bondage of sin as well as deliverance from the work of the Evil One can only come from the One who must be divine. Only such a One could redeem Israel or anyone in the nations.

Some worry that Israel has fallen never to rise again (Hos 14:1; Jer 8:4), but Isaiah answers that the Lord will "cleanse the bloodstains from Jerusalem by a spirit of judgment and a spirit of fire" (Isa 4:4). Only Messiah could cleanse the sin of "those who are left in Zion," who "will be called holy, all who are recorded among the living" [or: "are written to life"] (Isa 4:3).

Another debate breaks out over whether these Jewish people must believe "before" they are restored to their own land or does their restoration take place prior to their conversion? Ezekiel seems to answer the question in Ezekiel 36:24-27. "For I will take you out of the nations; I will gather you from all the countries and bring you back into your own land. [Then] I will sprinkle clean water on you, and you will be clean; I will cleanse you from all impurities and from all your idols. I will give you a new heart and a new spirit... I will put my Spirit in you..."

The sprinkling of clean water is not a reference to sanctification, because it happens before conversion. Rather here it is a reference to judgment, just as Isaiah 4:4 noted that the filth of the daughter of Zion is removed by "a spirit of judgment" and "a spirit of fire." Israel will experience a furnace of suffering to burn all the dross out of them (Ezek 22:18; Jer 30:3-7), but God's anger will not endure forever.

SUMMARY

Messiah is presented in four aspects: 1) a royal aspect, 2) a servant aspect, 3) a truly human aspect and 4) a divine aspect. Each completes the full portrait of Messiah and shares one of the emphases with each one of the four Gospels in the New Testament. The presentation of these aspects in the Tanak were given so that when Yeshua appeared, he would be recognized as Messiah—just as the Bereans searched the Tanak to validate what the apostles were claiming about Jesus as the Messiah. Messiah remained the central figure and the focus of the ancient promise-plan that God continued to promote throughout the two testaments. Messiah has not, nor will he ever forget his ancient promise to the people and land of Israel as well as other nations. Messiah is currently ruling and reigning from the right hand of the Father, but soon he will rule and reign over all the earth from Mount Zion to complete what he declared from the beginning.

CHAPTER 4

THE DAVIDIC COVENANT AS A ROYAL GRANT TYPE OF COVENANT

2 SAMUEL 7:1-29

When the Philistines, the perpetual hostile people living in the five cities on the southeastern Canaanite shores along the Mediterranean Sea, heard that David had been installed as king In Israel, they came out "in full force" (2 Sam 5:17; 1 Chron 14:8-16) to search for him. But when David learned that the Philistines were spread out in the Valley of Rephaim (a piece of fertile land west and southwest of Jerusalem), he inquired of the LORD as to what he should do (2 Sam 5:18). The Lord's answer was that he was to go and attack them and the LORD would hand them over to him (2 Sam 5:19).

David therefore attacked the Philistines at "Baal Perazim" and soundly defeated them (2 Sam 5:20). In fact, so resounding was David's victory, that the Philistines left the battle site in such a haste that they forgot to take their idols and gods along with them, so

David picked up these lifeless idols as captives—presumably to burn them as required by the LORD (1 Chron 14:12).

The Philistines returned to the Valley of Rephaim a second time to attack David, and when David again asked the LORD whether he should attack them, the LORD instructed him to circle around behind the Philistines to attack them from their rear guard when he heard the sound of marching in the tops of the Balsam trees. Once more David handily mowed down these foreign Philistine troops "all the way from Gibeon to Gezer," which was about 15 miles from Gibeon (2 Sam 5:24-25). With these victories, God gave David a season of rest from his enemies, which allowed him to experience a most climactic moment in the theology of the Bible, for God gave this new king what is known throughout Scripture as a "Royal Grant type of Treaty," which is usually referred to as "The Davidic Covenant." In fact, this covenant appears in both 2 Samuel 7:1-29 and I Chronicles 17:1-27, and it constitutes not only the highlights of these books, but the Davidic Covenant also stands as one of the four mountain peaks in the Tenak (=the Old Testament). The four mountain tops in the Old Testament are: (1) "the Edenic Covenant" in Genesis 3:15; (2) "the Abrahamic Covenant" in Genesis 12:2-3 and 15:1-6, (3) "the Davidic Covenant" just mentioned in 2 Samuel 7:1-29 and 1 Chronicles 17:1-27, and (4) "the New Covenant" in Jeremiah 31:31-34.

It is significant to note that this third mountain peak, "the Davidic Covenant" received more attention in the Hebrew Bible than any other section in the Bible except perhaps "the Sinaitic Covenant" given by Moses. The Davidic Covenant became one of the most frequently cited messages; according to some counts there are over forty individual texts in the Old Testament that appeal to this Davidic Covenant! Even among the Dead Sea Scrolls, there is a midrash on 2 Samuel 7:10b-14 written by the Qumran community, which pointed to numerous messianic allusions found in this text and throughout the Old Testament. This trend became even more pronounced in the New Testament that explored this text to its fullest extent in the further development of God's promise-plan for the people of Israel and the world.

A CONDITIONAL OR A ROYAL GRANT TYPE OF COVENANT?

There are a number of interpreters, both liberal and evangelical, who have argued that the Davidic Covenant was a "Conditional Covenant." But a larger number of interpreters have noted that from the middle of the second millennium onwards there existed another type of political treaty that was known as the "Royal Grant Treaty," which was very similar to the Davidic Covenant. In the royal grant treaty, the king or master of his subject vassal, emphasized the promissory nature of the gifts bestowed from the ruler to his vassal or subject nation. This, of course, is exactly what we find when we observe that Yahweh, the King of kings, promised his gifts to the patriarchs and to David, including the gift of the land of Canaan, the gift of numerous descendants or seed, and the divine blessings from God himself. David did not have conditions or obligations placed on him in order to receive these gifts from this royal grant treaty; the gifts and promises were unconditional.

It is surprising that nowhere in either the 2 Samuel 7 or the 1 Chronicles 17 passage is there any mention of the word "covenant," yet the chapter is almost universally recognized as Yahweh's Covenant with David. Its similarities to the royal grant types of treaties also becomes another reason for treating it as a covenant.

The Hittites also exhibited another type of treaty known as a "Suzerain Treaty" type, in which the Sovereign monarch promised protection along with other benefits given to the vassal or subject nation providing the subjects would observe the obligations the sovereign placed on them. But this obligatory nature of this type of treaty was the feature that did not appear in the Davidic Covenant.

The Background for the Davidic Covenant – 2 Samuel 7:1-3

David's life story is fascinating, for it relates how he ascended from being a local shepherd taken from the rural town of Bethlehem to becoming king over a people who were called by God to walk in his paths and in the light of his word. The opening words of 2 Samuel 7 emphasized the term "king" three times in three successive verses (7:1-3). Such a high calling from the LORD became more than a key reason why David began to show his gratitude to God by declaring his intention to build a Temple for the honor and glory of the LORD in Jerusalem (7:2). Now that David had finished building a palace for himself and since the Ark of the Covenant still rested in a tent since the days of Moses for over four hundred years, David thought the time had come for him to show his deep appreciation for all God had done for him. David desired to build a temple for the LORD.

When David's prophet, named Nathan, heard about David's new building plans to erect a Temple to the LORD, he encouraged him to do all that was in his heart. But Nathan spoke, as it were, off his cuff, and did not speak in the name and on the authority of the LORD, as he was supposed to do when he spoke prophetically. That night God appeared in Nathan in a dream and corrected his mis-speaking—David was not to build that Temple to the Lord (7:4).

God's Correction of Nathan's Blunder – 7:4-17

Nathan was told to speak in the name of the Lord to David and ask him this question: "Are you the one to build me a house to dwell in?" (7:5). The LORD went on in 7:8 to remind David how he had taken him from following sheep in the pasture to be a prince over all men. Then, from 7:9 on in this chapter, the LORD promised he would fulfill the following gifts and promises in the life of David:

"I will make you a great name, like the name of the great ones of the earth,

"I will appoint a place for my people Israel.

"I will plant them so that they may dwell in their own place a be disturbed no more.

"I will give you rest from all your enemies.

"I will make you a house.

"I will raise up your offspring after you, who shall come from your body.

"I will establish [your descendants'] kingdom."

"I will build a house for my name.

"I will establish your throne forever.

"I will be a Father to [your son].

"I will discipline [your son] with the rod of men.... but my steadfast love will not depart from him."

It is especially noteworthy that the LORD promised David to: (1) build him into a dynasty ("house"), (2) to give him a Throne, and (3) to establish a kingdom that would last forever (7:11b, 13, 16). Even though David is told he will not be allowed to build a Temple for the LORD, he was told instead that God would make a "house" out of him—David would found a Davidic dynasty from his seed in a ruling house that would last forever (1 Kgs 2:24). Just as the LORD had promised to Abraham and to his son that he would continue that line of descent forever, so David and his son and their sons' sons were promised the same gift into the future. For both Abraham and David, this "seed" would come from their own bodies (7:14; Gen 15:4; 17:7-10, 19). In Abraham's case, his son who would start that line was Isaac, but in David's case that son was Solomon. It is very important that we notice that the word for "seed" in Hebrew, Greek, and English is always a collective noun and therefore it can refer either to a single person, or to the whole group, as the solitary meaning or single sense of that word. The apostle Paul made this same point when he bluntly stated in Galatians 3:16 that the word given to Abraham and David was not a plural noun "seeds," but "seed," which meant preeminently that one person, who was Yeshua (Jesus), the Messiah, yet it also referred to all who trusted and believed in

Yeshua as well. These texts also repeatedly stress that this promise of the coming Messiah was an eternal and everlasting promise from God. Notice the word "forever" is repeated in 2 Samuel 7 seven times (7:13b, 16a, 16b, 24, 25, 29a, 29b, not to overlook the numerous other places where the same emphasis appears, such as in 1 Kgs 2:23, 45; 1 Chron 22:10; Ps 89:4. Even 2 Cor 6:18 and Heb 1:5 understood the words of 2 Sam 7:14a) as indicating a Messianic and Christological sense. Moreover, this Messianic sense and meaning 2 Samuel 7:14 was also portrayed in the Dead Sea Scrolls (4Q174), where the word "seed" was also understood in a collective sense—the "son" was Yeshua.

A further proof of God's care and love can be seen in the promise of Yeshua's resurrection from the dead in Isaiah 53:3, which was cited in Acts 13:34 where God declared that his love would never be removed from his loving kindness to David, but it would endure forever (1 Kgs 8:26; 1 Chron 17:23; 2 Chron 1:9; Ps 89:37).

David's Gracious Prayer to the LORD – 7:18-29

David, after hearing the prophesied word from Nathan, went into the tent he had pitched for the Ark of God as a humbled man (7:18). He began his prayer with a question that emphasized his utter humility, for he asked: "Who am I?" which was similar to the way Moses had addressed the LORD when he had been called by God to lead Israel out of the land of the most powerful country known to the world at that time (Exod 3:11).

David addressed the LORD as "Adonai Yahweh," a unique divine name which the NIV gave the rendering of "Sovereign LORD." David used this distinctive name for the LORD seven times in his prayer (7:18, 19[bis], 20, 22, 28, 29). Interestingly enough, that was the same name of address that Abraham had used in the Abrahamic Covenant (Gen 15:2, 8), which in both texts was surely meant to connect the two covenants in the same divine plan. That name for our LORD, "Adonai Yahweh," does not appear elsewhere in the two books of Samuel and it only appears in Moses' prayer in Deuteronomy 3:24 and 9:26, in Joshua's prayer in Joshua 7:7; in Gideon's prayer in Judges 6:22 and in Samson's prayer in Judges 16:28. Thus, our LORD is recognized as Sovereign LORD who is the giver of his covenant to his men who are his gifted vassals.

As David offered his prayer while sitting in the tent that housed the ark of the Covenant, he acknowledged the Lord's presence and all the promises and gifts for him as he spoke of the future of his dynasty. Moreover, what God gave to David was nothing less than "a charter for all humanity" (7:19b). This phrase was at the heart of what God was promising, for it was the *torat ha'adam,* i.e., "the instruction/charter for all mankind," yet translators continued to insist on an impossible translation of something like "Is this your usual way of dealing with man?" Recent translators have slowly begun to rectify this mistake in which those who had chosen the misinterpreted words had missed the heart of the Gospel and the Promise-Plan of God.

David continued in his prayer to describe the LORD as altogether unique and beyond any legitimate comparisons known to mortals (7:22). This matchless LORD had done three great things for his people Israel: (1) he had redeemed them, (2) he had made a name for himself in the midst of this people, and (3) he had performed great and awesome miracles (7:23). What is more, the LORD had driven out the enemy nations with their idols, just as he had miraculously delivered Israel from Egypt (7:23b). Israel was now established as his own people, and he had become their God (7:24).

2 Samuel 7:25-29 highlights his promise to David and his people through whom he had decided to bless not only David and his people, but all the nations of the earth, and thus show the world the sign of his greatness (7:26). The LORD himself would establish this word. Thus, David ended his prayer by asking God to bless the house of his servant David and to grant that this blessing would be forever.

SUMMARY

The Philistines made a desperate, but final attack, on David when they heard he had been installed as king in Israel. God delivered David from these assaults and gave him a period of rest from all his enemies. Then, God gave "the Davidic Covenant" to this newly installed king over Israel in 2 Samuel 7:1-29 and in 1 Chronicles 17:1-27. It is one of the four mountain peaks of God's Promise-Plan and lovingkindness to Israel and to the world; this Davidic Covenant is cited elsewhere in Scripture over some forty times, which is more than any other block of text except the "Sinaitic Covenant" given to Moses. While the 2 Samuel passage does not call it a "Covenant," it is none-the-less understood as a covenant by interpreters of many different theological stripes. At the heart of this text, is the promise that God would make of David a dynasty, a throne, and a kingdom that would last forever, and which would be the "instruction/charter for all humanity."

CHAPTER 5

THE HUMILIATION AND TRIUMPH OF MESSIAH

PSALM 22:1-31

INTRODUCTION

Have you ever felt like the disciples of our Lord Jesus when they asked him: "Lord, teach us to pray?" Perhaps that is just why our Lord had David contribute so many of the Psalms to our Bibles, so we could know how to pray! Our Lord wanted us to be schooled in the joy of worship and the call to pray. But some of the Psalms are just as easily classified as songs of joy, praise, and thanksgiving, for the songs of joy to our Lord are just as much a part of worship as is our praying to him.

David was gifted by the Lord with the genius of a poet, a wisdom that comes from God, and a skill in playing the harp. It is not hard to imagine him out on the hills of Judah watching over the sheep that belonged to his father singing his heart out loud to the Lord.

With the beauty of creation all around him and the solitude and quietness of those hours alone with the sheep, his heart and life were comforted as the Lord led him and guided him as he composed songs and prayers which expressed the joy and desires of his heart.

Perhaps you too, occasionally have had moments similar to those David experienced when you found yourself all alone out in splendor of the woods or meadows that God had furbished, haven't you? Whether you had a good voice or couldn't even hold a tone on your own in a bucket, the sheer joy of being alone while sensing the presence of God led you to burst out loud in a song filled with joy, thanksgiving, and homage to your Lord.

The book of Psalms expressed many of David's deepest passions for God and his deep desire to walk and talk with the Living God, for he is the author of almost half of the 150 Psalms. Others later joined David in the same heart-felt desire to praise God such as the sons of Korah, Ethan, Heman, and Asaph. But we will focus on David's Psalms in Book I in this study. But first, let us take a peek at the whole book of Psalms.

THE BOOK OF PSALMS

The 150 chapters of the book of Psalms were composed over a period of some five hundred years, roughly from the time of David around 1000 BC until the times coming right after the Babylonian exile, that began the year Jerusalem fell in 586 BC. Yet for too long now, the book of Psalms has been treated merely as a sort of hodge-podge of prayers, songs, and poems randomly connected to each other with no planned pattern of arrangement or purpose discernable in the whole book—at least that is what most had concluded!, But that is beginning to change now with books like *The Flow of the Psalms: Discovering their Structure and Theology* (by O. Palmer Robertson, Phillipsburg, NJ: P & R, 2015). Thus, after centuries of scholarly judgment that such a search for some kind of pattern of organization in Psalms was plainly an "unattainable end," there now comes a beautiful discussion and announcement of what others had said was just impossible.

Robertson argues that the flow in the book of Psalms goes like this: Book I (Pss 1–41) begins with the "confrontation" between the wicked and righteous, that marks all of history until the consummation. Book II (42–72) speaks to the animosity between the two seeds on earth (Gen 3:15) with a "communication" for all to join in the worship of the Lord. In Book III (Pss 73–89), Israel experiences "devastation" from the hands of the nations round about them. But in Book IV (Pss 90–106), the people of the Lord gain "maturation" as they realize the Lord reigns even though they have been displaced in foreign countries. Book V (Pss 107–150), finally, shows how God's people will experience the "consummation" as they shout "Hallelu-YAH." So let's dig into this book, especially those sections that come from David, and see what the flow of its structure and theology reveals.

First off, as we have just noticed, there are five books in the Psalms. They are:

Book I: Psalms 1–41	Doxology 41:13	(41 Psalms)
Book II: Psalms 42–72	Doxology 72:18-19	(31 Psalms)
Book III: Psalms 73–89	Doxology 89:52	(17 Psalms)
Book IV: Psalms 90–106	Doxology 106:48	(17 Psalms)
Book V: Psalms 107–150	Doxology 150	(44 Psalms)

How the Structure of the Book of Psalms Is Built

Importantly Psalms 1 and 2 are foundational to any discussion of the substance of the rest of Psalter, for they introduce all that will follow in the remaining chapters. In his recent book, Palmer Robertson calls these two Psalms the "Two Poetic Pillars" that both anticipate and permeate the rest of the Psalter. The feature: the Torah and the Messiah; or to say it in another way: the Law and the Gospel.

These two "poetic pillars" stand both at our entrance into the book of Psalms and act as a guide as to what we are going to find in this wonderful book mostly composed under inspiration of the Spirit by David!

Psalm 1 begins with the contrast between the "wicked" (a term occurring about 90 times in the whole book) and "righteous" (a term occurring about 50 times in the book) as the descent of the ungodly person is traced in this first Psalm. This Psalm taught that the "wicked:"

"walk in step with the [unrighteous],
stand in the way that sinners take, [and]
sit in the company of mockers" (Ps 1:1, NIV, 2011)

On the other hand, the "righteous" have taken an altogether different course. They, instead:

Delight in the law of the LORD, [and]
Meditate on it day and night. (Ps 1:2, NIV 2011).

The contrast could not be sharper between the wicked and righteous. Throughout the Psalms, this contrast continues and so the confrontation of the enemies of God and his word from the opposing sides in the contest of life. Robertson (in the book mentioned above) concluded that at two crucial points in the structure of Psalms, additional Torah Psalms reappear: Psalm 19 and Psalm 119, thus emphasizing how central the law was to the whole plan of Psalms.

However, here is a second major theme to this book of Psalms: the person of God's Messiah (Ps 2). The wicked and the nations of the world are not pleased at all with his appearance, for "the kings of the earth rise up and the rulers band together against the LORD and against his Anointed" (Ps 2:2). But all their protesting continues to be useless, for God has already decreed in the Davidic Covenant about David: "You are my son" (2 Sam 7:14; Ps 2:7). God the Father has given to his "son" "the nations [as his] inheritance" and "the ends of the earth" [as his] "possession" (Ps 2:8). The kings of the earth and all the rulers of this world would be well advised to "Serve the

LORD with fear" (11a) to "do obeisance to the Son" (12), for he is Lord over everything. Robertson points out four major themes are found in Psalm 2 and the rest of the Psalms that come from the Davidic Covenant (2 Sam 7 and 1Chron 17): (1) the Lord's kingship over all nations (Pss 2:1; 10:16; 47:2), (2) the place of the Lord's rule will be in Mount Zion of Jerusalem (Pss 2:6; 9:11; 48:2), (3) The permanent establishment of David's throne (Pss 2:7; 18:50; 89:3-4, 20), and (4) there will be a merger of David's throne with the Lord's throne (Pss 2:6; 11:4; 20:2, 6; 53:2).

The two opening Psalms, then, set out in condensed form the overarching message of the Psalter—the law and the Messiah. David is cited in the ancient titles of Book I of the Psalter as the author of 37 of these Psalms. The Apostle Peter in Acts 4:25 acknowledged that David was the author of Psalm 2, even though that Psalm did not include this information in its title. Two other Psalms, 10 and 33 are without titles, but Psalm 10 is joined to Psalm 9 by completing the acrostic poem begun in Psalm 9, which is also attributed to David.

Only five Psalms in Book I have no singular personal pronoun in the text: "I" (Pss 12, 14, 15, 24, 29) creating a kind of direct application. This is an important point, for these "I- psalms" draw each reader irrespective of the Psalmist historical-cultural setting to hear God's anointed Messianic king, David speaking to them. But these "I-psalms" also simultaneously function in a similar way for each member of God's Messianic Kingdom, as these psalms teach us how to act and pray in very similar situations of life. Thus, as David deals with the tragedies in his own life, for example such as his son Absalom leading a revolt against him in Psalm 3 (the rebellious son syndrome), so all God's people can call on God in similar situations for his intervention and help from the Lord.

Also, in Book I, it is important to note the key role that Psalms 18 and 19 play as Messianic Psalms. They are coupled with a Torah Psalm in Book I, which thereby mirrors the two opening Psalms 1 and 2. Psalm 18 represents 2 Samuel 22 with hardly any modification in its title to the psalm, for it indicates that David composed this piece "when the LORD delivered him from the hand of his enemies and from the hand of Saul." Its placement in the Psalter attached to Torah a Psalm appears deliberate as if it continues to carry out the key themes of the opening two foundational pillars of Psalms 1 and 2. Consequently, once David is securely established as the messianic "king," and as the Lord's "anointed", indeed as his "son" (Ps 2:2, 6, 7, 12), the Psalmist is now free to use this terminology about his kingship freely after Psalms 18–19 (Pss 20:6, 9; 21:1, 7; 28:8).

Even more interesting is the fact that now the pyramid of five kingship psalms also appears right after Psalm 18–19. The five psalms of 20–24 are strategically placed so that they can respond to the messianic Psalm 18. Thus, if Psalm 22 is at the apex of this "kingship pyramid" of five psalms, Psalms 20–21 begin the pyramid by presenting David's prayers that call for the Lord's intervention to uphold the Davidic kingship. These two psalms are balanced off by two psalms that conclude the pyramid (Psalm 23–24), which present assurances that God himself would show how glorious and triumphant the Lord's own kingship would be. Psalm 22 is at the apex of the pyramid as a mediating psalm, joining the Davidic kingship to the Lord's ultimate kingship over everything.

Thus the 41 psalms of the first Davidic collection are divided into two sections: Psalms 3–17 and Psalms 18–41, while joined together by a messianic psalm (18) and a torah psalm (19). Meanwhile, teaching and instruction, which are the essence of the torah psalm are found in passages such as Psalm 25:4-5 ("Show me your ways, O LORD, teach me your paths; guide me in your truth and teach me"), Psalm 32:8 ("I will instruct you and teach you in the way you should go; I will counsel you and watch over you"), and Psalm 34:11 ("Come, my children, listen to me; I will teach you the fear of the LORD"). So, the teaching part is joined to the messianic part as the foundation for understanding the rest of the Psalter. But let us focus on Pslam 22 as the apex psalm in the five-kinship pyramid of Psalms 20–24:

Text: Psalm 22:1-31

Focal Point: "Praise him! .... Revere him! .... For he has not despised or scorned the suffering of [His] afflicted one ... but he has listened to His cry for help." (Ps 22:23b-24).

Title: The Triumph over Suffering in the Humiliation of God's Messianic King

Homiletical Keyword: Questions and Assurances

Interrogative: WHAT? (ARE THE QUESTIONS AND THE ASSURANCES God gives to David and to us?)

Outline:

- ***I. Often We are Made Anxious by the Silences of God – 22:1-5***
- ***II. Often We are Scorned by Men but Assured by God – 22:6-11***
- ***III. Often We are Intimidated by Enemies but Delivered by God – 22:12-21***
- ***IV. Always We are Jubilant Over the Victory Wrought by God – 22:22-31***

The Lesson:

I. Often We Are Made Anxious By The Silences Of God – 22:1-5

Suffering was not an unexpected path for David to experience, nor is it an unexpected path for our Lord himself or for the followers of the Lord. This whole psalm must have been on the mind of our Lord during his trial of the suffering of the cross, for the so-called fourth word from the cross ("My God, My God, why have you forsaken me?" Ps 22:1) and the so-called sixth word from the cross ("It is finished," Ps 22: 31c; John 19:30) both come from Psalm 22. The assignment of titles to a book or work, are more of a modern phenomenon, but in ancient days it was typical to refer to a piece of writing by the first or opening words in its first line, which is what happened as our Lord cried out these words on the cross: "My God, my God, why have you forsaken me?".

In fact, our Lord posed four questions to the Father as he hung on the cross:

> Why have you forsaken me? 22:1a
> Why are you so far from saving me? 22:1b
> Why [are you] so far from the cries of my anguish? 22:1c
> Why do you not answer? 22:2a

The enemies of our Lord had [mockingly] just quoted from verse 8 ("He trusts in the LORD, ... Let the LORD rescue him." (Matt 27:43)

However, only those who have a personal relationship with the Lord can also cry out as our Lord did here, "My, God, my God." That, of course is where we should put the proper emphasis on these words (i.e., on the final word, "my"), otherwise they turn into a form of swearing! The Hebrew text would make the same point, for it is Eli, Eli, with ending syllable "-i" representing the pronoun "my" as being emphasized. Furthermore, our Lord had predicted that the hour was coming when all his disciples would scatter, however he would not be alone, "for his Father was with him" (John 16:32). Only those who forsake God need worry about his abandonment of them (2 Chron 12:5; 15:2; 24:20). In Matthew's Gospel (27:46), the "why?" (in "why have you forsaken me?") asks the reason for this temporary forsaking (Greek: *hinati*; Hebrew, *lammah*), but in Mark's Gospel (15:34) the "why?" of Jesus asks for the design of what God is doing (Greek, *eis ti*, Hebrew, *lema*). The older commentator Franz Delitzsch commented on these different interrogatives by asserting: the element common to David's case, our case and Messiah's is this: behind the wrath felt, there is hidden the love of God which holds fast and maintains our fellowship with God.... Surely, as others have commented, there is a mystery here that no human mind can fathom, but let the one who has taken comfort in the fact that Jesus suffered each particular type of temptation we suffer and the one who has been disappointed by the words, "without sin" (Heb 4:15), and who therefore feels this radically limits his identification with us consider this: Christ has plumbed the depths of trial and suffering far deeper than any human mind has ever comprehended.

However, we are reassured by the answers that come in verses 3-5.
Our God is holy, so our appeal to him will not be forgotten.
Israel trusted him in the past and was not disappointed.
Israel cried to God and was delivered.

II. Often We are Scorned by Men but Assured by God – 22:6-11

Each of the words found in verse 6 are paralleled by similar or the same words found in Isaiah.

"I am a worm" (cf. Isa 41:14)
"and not a man" (cf. Isa 53:3)
"a reproach of Men" (cf. Isa 52:14)
"despised by the people" (cf. Isa 49:7).

So, the enemies of the Lord and the wicked continued by mocking and insulting the Lord as they shook their heads against him (Ps 22:6-7). They lambasted him by urging him to come down off the cross and save them and himself (22:8), but the Lord gave this reassuring answer in Psalm 22:9 –10:

God brought him through birth,
God protected him during his early years,
God has always been his God.

While this text mentions his "mother" twice, it never mentions his earthly "father." On the grounds of his fellowship with God, his cry for help finds expression in the words: "Do not be far from me" (22:11). God's comfort, then, was greater than the scorn and mocking that came from sinners.

III. Often We are Intimidated by Enemies but Delivered By God! – 22:12-21

The psalmist likens his enemies to be as vicious and ravenous as bulls and lions (12-13). He describes his condition as one that is poured out like water (14a), whose bones are all out of joint (14b), whose heart is like wax (14c) and one whose strength is gone (14d). His tongue sticks to the roof of his mouth (15a) and he feels he is lying in the dust of death (15b).

Moreover, his humiliation is so great that he feels encircled and like one who is being hounded by a pack of dogs (16a). They have pierced his hands and his feet (16b) and he is being stared at (17b). They even divide up his clothes (18a) and gamble over personally owning his robe (18b). But his prayer, nevertheless, is that the Lord would not be far from him (19a) and that he would come quickly and deliver him (19b). The Lord would deliver him from the sword, dogs, lions, and bulls (20-21). Calvin commented that for those who might say that the Father failed to come to the aid of his son, he and we would answer that he more mightily delivered him than if the danger had merely been averted, for to raise one from the dead is surely much more powerful than to merely turn evil away from one's side.

IV. Always We are Jubilant Over the Victory Wrought by God – 22:22-31

The fact that our Lord delivered Christ is triumphantly set forth at the end of this kingship Psalm 22. The exaltation comes from Israel first in verses 22-26 and then from the nations at large in verses 27-29b. The call is for those who reverently fear the name of the Lord to "praise him" and to "revere him." The reason for this rejoicing is clear: God has not despised or scorned Christ's suffering, nor has he hidden his face from his troubles.

But that rejoicing is matched by the praise that comes from the "ends of the earth" (27a). "All the families of the nations will bow down before our Lord" (27b). Again, the reason is given in verse 28, because "dominion belongs to the LORD, and he rules over the nations" (28).

Three times in the Bible, the theology of fulfillment and completion has come ("It is finished"): (1) In the beginning, God put a stop day (*a Shabbat*, "a Sabbath," i.e., a "stop day" in Gen 1:31) to his creative work, (2) on the cross, once again our Lord said the great work of our redemption was completed as he uttered the words: "It is finished" (John 19:30), and (3) at the conclusion of the end times of history, God will once more say "It is done" (Rev 21:6). Praise him for concluding all things well, whether the creation of all things, our salvation, or the wrap up of history!

SUMMARY

The book of Psalms is not a random collection of prayers and praises to God but it is built on the foundational themes of the law and the Messiah so the Psalms will teach us both how to pray and direct us to the Messiah Whom we owe our love, trust, and obedience. David is the composer of well over half of the 150 Psalms. He is also the one to whom God pledged to give to his descendants an everlasting kingdom, dominion, throne, and dynasty to which Christ himself would ascend in the fullness of time. Psalm 22 is one of the great highlights in the Psalter as it predicted the death and resurrection of Messiah, Yeshua our Redeemer and coming King.

CHAPTER 6

THE EXTENT OF THE RULE AND REIGN OF MESSIAH

PSALM 72:1-18

J. Barton Payne asserts, "The greatest block of predictive material concerning the Savior to be found anywhere in the Old Testament," is in the book of Psalms.[23] He found 101 verses in the Psalms of direct Messianic prophecies in thirteen different Psalms. Other writers tended to be more conservative in their estimates, such as the Lutheran commentator H. C. Leupold, who limited the number of Messianic passages in the book of Psalms to four: Psalms 22, 45, 72, 110.[24] At the other extreme was St. Augustine, who unfairly treated every Psalm as if it were Messianic. But his approach violated the basic rules of exegesis, for it is better to rely on the straightforward claims of the text itself than to apply a spiritualized or allegorical sense to the words as argued by the Church father named Origin.

In our treatment of Messiah in the Psalms,[25] we argued for thirteen messianic Psalms: 2, 16, 22, 40, 45, 68, 69, 72, 89, 109,

23 J. Barton Payne, *Encyclopedia of Biblical Prophecy* (New York: Harper and Row, 1973), 257.

24 H. C. Leupold, *Exposition of Psalms* (Grand Rapids: Baker, 1974), 21-23.

25 Kaiser, *The Messiah in the Old Testament*, 92-135.

110, 118, and 132. This is very similar to the list given by James E. Smith,[26] though e argued for sixteen such Psalms. Thus, he added Psalms 8, 78:1-2 [sic], and 102.

As we have often described these Psalms, arranged in the order of the predictions made in the life of Messiah, the following suggested order is as follows:

David's Greater Son, Messiah – Psalms 89, 132
The Rejection of Messiah – Psalm 118
The Betrayal of Messiah – Psalms 69, 109
The Death and Resurrection of Messiah – Psalms 16, 22
The Written Plan and Marriage of Messiah – Psalms 40, 45
The Triumph of Messiah – Psalms 2, 68, 72, 110

The author of Psalm 72 is said in 72:1 to be king "Solomon." Therefore, it is most significant that this Psalm is also known as a direct Messianic Psalm because it uses the future tense throughout the Psalm and also because of the frequent use of the figure of speech called hyperbole, which even King Solomon, who wrote this Psalm according to its ancient heading, could not have personally fulfilled despite all his personal glory. Instead, Solomon's reign can supply only the imagery, language, and line of descent through which the one and only proper occupant of the throne; the future Messiah Who can fill that position in the proposed peaceful and prosperous rule and reign that is to come in that future day.

Psalm 72 is one of the "Royal," or "Kingship Psalms," which Hermann Gunkel (1862–1932) described as such in his *Die Psalmen* (1926–28).[27] Gunkel had proposed ten Royal Psalms, according to their literary forms: Psalms 2, 20, 21, 28, 45, 72, 101, 109, 132 and 144:1-11, but it did not seem that Psalms 101 or 110 met his own criteria. Much later, John H. Eaton used the criteria that Gunkel

---

26 James E. Smith, *What the Bible Teaches About the Promised Messiah* (Nashville, TN: Thomas Nelson, 1993), 90-209.

27 Much of the material that follows is an expansion of my article, "Psalm 72: An Historical and Messianic Current Example of Antiochene Hermeneutical *Theoria*," *JETS* 52/2 (June 2009):257-70.

argued for in identifying two of his Royal Psalms, by showing that they had a Davidic superscription, as he went on to develop some twenty-four additional characteristics for this category of Royal of Kingship Psalms, resulting in a list of fifty-four Royal Psalms, which he then added to Gunkel's original list of ten Royal Psalms.

Surprisingly, however, nowhere in the New Testament is Psalm 72 quoted or treated as a Messianic Psalm. Yet, despite this fact, where for some, such a fact would severely limit its Messianic identity for those who argue solely from a Christotelic, or apostolic approach, an approach that gives what these interpreters hope is the permission to "reinterpret" the text from a New Testament standpoint. Nevertheless, so clear is the picture of "the king" described in this Psalm and so extensive and so far-reaching are the boundaries of his rule and reign, not to mention the similarities seen between this Psalm and Isaiah 11:1-5 or Isaiah 60–62, that one cannot deny that Psalm 72 also is Messianic and indeed a Royal Psalm.

Another clue to its Messianic interpretation is the use of metaphoric and hyperbolic language that clearly extended the limits of the royal reign well beyond the boundaries of Israel and the times of Solomon, or any other Davidic king for that matter. It is this use of "hyperbolic" language that brings us to a dialogue with the "Antiochene School," which was founded by Lucian of Antioch (AD 312), and who was followed by such imposing names as Theodoret of Mopsuestia (AD 350–428), Jerome (AD 347–420) and John Chrysostom (AD 347–407) in this same line of thought.

The Antiochene School established the model for what they called the "Theoria" view, which meant in the Greek the "sight," "insight," "vision," or the lining up of what had happened in the past with an analogous final event in the distant future, so that the past event and the coming future event could be said to be one and unified in their single meaning, even though they might describe two separate events: one in the past, and the other to come in similar, but future fulfillments. The work of Bradley Nassif's Fordham

University doctoral dissertation[28] on the method of *theoria,* has been especially helpful to me in analyzing this practice of *theoria* in the Psalms.

The Antiochians of Syria were well known as opponents of the the allegorical or spiritual method of interpreting the Scriptures in Alexandria. The Antiochian School grounded all their meanings from Scripture to be grounded in the historical reality of the past, which often served as a mirror by which one could see the future lined up analogically with the same single meaning of both the past and the future, so that the past and the distant future were part and parcel of the same single vision and shared features with each other.

It was "Julian of Eclanum," who seems to have best learned the principle of *theoria* from Theodore while living with him from AD 421–428, after he had been exiled from Italy. Theodore demonstrated the method of *Theoria* in the way the Apostle Paul used Hosea 1:10 ("And it will come about that, in the place where it is said to them, 'You are my people,' It will be said to them, 'You are sons of the living God.'") in Romans 9:26, therefore Julian taught:

> The apostle wants to show us which rule we must follow in the interpretation of the prophetic books. It is this: That when [we hear the prophets] speaking about the Jews, [and] something is promised that goes behind the small circle of people, yet we see it partly fulfilled in that nation, we know from *theoria (per theoriam)* that the promise is given for all people.... It will not be appropriate to say that the recall from the Babylonian captivity is predicted according to history, and the liberty given by Christ [is] according to allegory. No. The prophet predicted both things together at one time, jointly *(cum sermo propheticus solide utrumque promiserit)* in order that the mediocrity of the first fulfillment would predict the abundance of the second ... So what Hosea was saying about

28 Bradley Nassif, "Antiochene *Theoria* in John Chrysostom's Exegesis" (PhD dissertation, Fordham University, New York, 1991).

> the Babylonian times, Paul [likewise] attributes to the facts of the Savior.[29]

This approach to interpreting the Old Testament prophets is very similar to the method used by Willis J. Beecher's method of "Generic Interpretation." Beecher did not use the term *theoria,* but he defined his parallel method of interpreting prophecy in this way:

> A generic prediction is one which regards an event as occurring in a series of parts, separated by intervals, and expresses itself in language that may apply indifferently to the nearest part, or to the remotest parts, or to the whole—in other words, a prediction which, in applying to the whole of a complex event also applies to ... its parts.[30]

This is not to say that the Antiochene School or Beecher were teaching "double meaning," or "double sense," as if the historic meaning meant one thing in the past and in the future fulfillment, it intended another meaning; instead, that is precisely what both were clearly trying to avoid. Therefore, they argued for one sense, one meaning, even though there often were multiple fulfillments of that same single meaning of the text that was shared "hyperbolically" or "analogically."

THE CANONICAL PLACEMENT OF PSALM 72

Several commentators have investigated why certain Psalms are placed on the "seams" or divisions of the five books of the Psalter. Furthermore, what patterns of organization can be discerned from the placement of the Psalms if there is one to be found at all.

29 Nassif, "Antiochene *Theoria,*" 55. Nassif cited it from the Latin in A Vaccari, "La '*theoria*' nella scula esegetica di antiochia," *Bib* 1 (1920):20-22. Nassif commissioned the English translation.

30 Willis J. Beecher. *The Prophets and the Promise* (1905; reprint Grand Rapids: Baker 1963, 1970), 130.

Walter Brueggemann and Patrick Miller[31] noted that the placement of Psalm 73, which appears at the beginning of Book III (Psalms 73–89), stands in juxtaposition to Psalm 72, a Psalm authored "by/for Solomon," that ends Book II in the Psalter. If this were done intentionally, which we believe they were, then why were the two Psalms placed back to back? If Psalm 73 is a sapiential, or wisdom Psalm, as most correctly contend, and Psalm 72 is a royal psalm, does the juxtaposition of the two Psalms have meaning and significance than what immediately meets the eye at first glance.

G. H. Wilson, argued for precisely that point when he claimed that there was a progression in the royal psalms placed at the seams of Books I–II of the Psalter. In these psalms it was possible to chart the rise and fall of the Davidic monarchy. Thus, for Wilson,[32] Psalm 2 marked the inauguration of the Davidic Covenant, while Psalm 72 marked its transition to a future line of Israelite kings, leaving Psalm 89 (at the end of Book III) to lament what had happened to the rejection of that line (even if it were only temporary from an evangelical point of view) of the Davidic kings. Some think this also explains why the Royal Psalms play such a small role in Books IV to V, when compared to their larger role in Books I–III.

Christopher Seitz[33] has taken this argument one step further. He proposed to view the Davidic House and kingship of God as portrayed in Psalms and Isaiah as being parallel to one another. Therefore, as the Davidic throne *recedes* into the background and then finally *disappears,* as it appears to do from the Fall of Jerusalem in 586 BC onwards, the kingship of God *rises* in prominence from there on out instead. Accordingly, Psalm 72 is to be viewed as a fading marker of the Davidic line, thereby allowing the emergence

31 Walter Brueggemann and Patrick D. Miller, "Psalm 73 as Canonical Marker," *JSOT* 72 (1996):45-56.

32 G. H. Wilson, "The Use of Royal Psalms at the 'Seams' of the Hebrew Psalter," *JSOT* 35(1986):85-94.

33 Christopher Seitz, "Royal Promises in the Canonical Books of Isaiah and Psalms," in *Isaiah in Scripture and the Church* (unpublished manuscript, 1994) referred to in Brueggemann and Miller, "Psalm 73," 51 n. 17.

of the Enthronement Psalms about God in Book IV (Pss 90–106) to take center stage.

It is directly in answer to this pitting the Davidic Dynasty opposite the coming enthronement of Messiah that makes a return to the Antiochian hermeneutic of *theoria* so useful. Instead of "reinterpreting," or contrasting the promised throne of David with the rule of Messiah, one can still insist on retaining the full historical setting and meaning of Psalm 72 with its centering on the Davidic kingship in the past, while noting that the Psalm's hyperbolic progression of a conscious enlargement of that concept involved a progress from the seminal idea as given to David and his house back then as it moved as one idea over into its final realization in the ultimate Davidic king, the Messiah who would come in the last day. The text itself will be the best place to test this thesis.

Text: Psalm 72:1-17

Focal Point: vv 7-8 "In his days the righteous will flourish; prosperity will abound till the moon is no more. He will rule from sea to sea and from the River [Euphrates] to the ends of the earth."

Title: "The Extent of Messiah's Rule and Reign"

Homiletical Keyword and Interrogative: CHARACTERISTICS. HOW? (to what extent should we characterize our enjoyment of the blessings of the kingdom promised to the Davidic-Messianic rule and reign?)

Teaching Aim: To show that Solomon was only one of many in the Davidic line who would be finally fulfilled in the world-wide rule and reign of Messiah.

Outline:

Characteristics:

I. By Observing How Righteous and Fair The Messiah is to All – 72:1-7

II. By Noting How Extensive and Beneficial The Messiah is to the Whole World – 72:8-14

III. By Sensing How Prosperous and Blessed Messiah is to All – 72:15-17

Expositional Commentary:

I. By Observing How Righteous and Fair The Messiah is to All – 1-7

I. Introduction:

Many have wanted to view Psalm 72 as composed in four poetic strophes based on what they perceive as four themes of the king's and Messiah's reign; the king's rule was described as being a reign that was: (1) righteous (72:1-7), (2) universal (Ps 72:8-11), (3) beneficial (72:12-14), and (4) perpetual (72:15-17). For example, James Smith argued for these same four qualities of Messiah's future reign.[34] But a better case was made by Charles A. Briggs for seeing only three strophes in this Psalm, each beginning with a prayer by Solomon in verses 1, 8, and 15.[35] In Brigg's view, the three prayers corresponded to Solomon's prayer for wisdom offered at Gibeon and his prayer at the dedication of the Temple. This seems to be the best division of the Psalm; therefore, the suggested exposition of this passage will follow that structure for our analysis of this text.

The imagery and content of this Psalm is prompted by the peaceful and prosperous reign of the grandest monarch Judah ever had, King Solomon. It is this historical reality that had served as the basis for anticipating a surpassing hyperbolic expression and a robust expansion of such a greater reign coming in the future, but which had only been seen in modest glimpses experienced now and again by the Davidic King Solomon. It is not as if Solomon cherished the wish that he in his person would finally epitomize, or even perhaps that he would be that coming Messianic person himself; rather, Solomon

34 James Smith. *What the Bible Teaches*, 195.

35 Charles A. Briggs, *Messianic Prophecy* (New York: Charles Scribner's Sons, 1889), 137-40.

speaks here as a prophet who anticipated one who would come after him and who would be greater than he ever was or ever could hope to be (cf. Matt 12:42).

Psalm 72 begins with a prayer to God that is signaled by its vocative form. "O Elohim!" "Elohim" was the divine name that embraced all nations and all of creation, along with all its creatures in its address, whereas "Yahweh" usually assumed a personal relationship with the people who were believers. Even though this Psalm may originally have been created for the earthly coronation ceremony of Solomon, as some correctly argue, nonetheless much of the content of the verses that follow exceed and extend well beyond that single setting, so that they could hardly be understood solely of any earthly monarch except by way of pure "hyperbole."[36] This, of course, was one of the reasons why Christians have treated this Psalm as Messianic as well as being one that historically refers to Solomon.

With this prayer, Solomon continued with a demand ("give," i.e., "endow," in the imperative mood) that Elohim would endow the king with the concept and gift of justice. The verbs used here are best understood as future tenses, rather than the jussive forms usually rendered as "may, or "let." These verbs request that God would indeed grant such a request to "a king" (Hebrew, *lemelek*), not "the king." The scope of this request is enlarged by making "a king" parallel to "a son of the king" (Hebrew, *leben melek*). The concern of the psalmist is for the whole royal house of David, as climaxed in Messiah himself, be gifted in the same way.

The only use made of the divine name in this whole psalm is "Elohim." Elohim was requested to endow the king with two divinely originated virtues: "God's justices" (note the rare plural) and God's "righteousness." The plural of the word "justice" probably signified justice in the fullest form of God's decisions and judgments, while the gift of his "righteousness" pointed to what was right, harmonious

36 So commented Mitchell Dahood. *Psalms, vol. 2:51-100*. Anchor Bible (Garden City, NY: Doubleday, 1968), 179.

and normal in all relations between God and mortals as determined by the character and attributes of God. This righteousness is mentioned three times in just three verses (1-3). It included the concept of God's law and the state of being in conformity with all that is good, excellent, and that which maintains what is "in-the-right" with the will and work of God. The hope expressed here is that this endowed king will continue to dispense these gifts for a long time to come.

It is at this point where the author's hyperboles begin to manifest themselves as extending over a duration of such a time of peace, prosperity, and divine vindication, and that they would extend "as long as the sun and as long as the moon last" (v 5). It is important to recall, however, that this very same concept of perpetuity is what had been promised specifically in an earlier word in the Davidic Covenant (2 Sam 7:13, 16).[37] The psalmist's prayer request, then, is that God would make happen all he had promised to David in the Davidic Covenant in that grand day when the Messiah will come!

In addition to these requests, the peace and prosperity of the kingly reign is likened to "rain falling on a mown field (v 6). This too is not an unexpected metaphor in a Davidic or Messianic context, for it has already been used of the refreshing effects of the future reign of a Davidic king in 2 Samuel 23:3b-4 ("When one rules over men in righteousness, when he rules in the fear of God, he is like ... the brightness after rain that brings the grass from the earth"). It is also worthy of special note that the fertility of any country or land is connected to the righteous rule and reign of a just and fair king. It is important to note how frequently the concepts of "rain," "growth," and "fertility" are linked with the concepts of "right," "righteousness," and "justice" in the Scriptures. These sets of attributes cannot be separated if peace, justice, and righteousness are expected to prevail in any country.

37 For further elaboration on this point, see Walter C. Kaiser, Jr., "The Blessing of David: The Charter for Humanity," in *The Law and the Prophets: Old Testament Studies in Honor of O.T. Allis*, ed. John H. Skilton (Phillipsburg, NJ: Presbyterian and Reformed, 1974), 298-318.

II. By Noting How Extensive And Beneficial Messiah Is To The Whole World -72:8-14

The extent of the just king's kingdom stretches from "sea to sea" and "from the River [Euphrates] to the ends of the earth" (v 8). This would cover everything from the Mediterranean Sea on the west of Israel to the uttermost sea on the earth, and from the Euphrates River (for so the Hebrew spelling here demands by its usage the Euphrates River) unto the ends of the earth—an obvious set of hyperboles! In part, there is also an allusion to the boundaries of the promised land (Exod 23:31, where it was announced that, "I will establish your borders from the Red Sea [Yam Suph] to the Sea of the Philistines [Mediterranean Sea] and from the desert to the River [Euphrates]"). However, the kingdom of Messiah will far exceed anything ever seen in the Judean line of kings in the past. Messiah's kingdom would reach the fringes of the civilized world, embracing the desert tribes, and it would even subjugate all "enemies," who would suffer defeat as they "lick[ed or bit] the dust" (v 9), as had been predicted against Satan himself in the earliest announcement of the Promise-Plan of God, later called the "Protoevangelium" in Genesis 3:14-15, and repeated for all the Davidic kings' enemies in Isaiah 49:23 and Micah 7:17a ("Nations .... will lick dust like a snake, like creatures that crawl on the ground").

But there is more: the reign of this righteous king would extend as we have seen thus far: (1) *geographically* from sea to sea, which is to say around the world; (2) *militarily* over all enemies opposing his reign; but now add to this that this reign would extend (3) *economically*, as tribute and gifts will be brought from all over the world (v 10); and (4) *politically*, so far as all potentates will come under this righteous king's rule and serve him (v 11). Nations far and near will come bringing gifts to him, much as the Magi did when Messiah first appeared in his first advent. Another example of the nations coming from abroad can be seen in the reference to "Tarshish" (v 10), long identified with Tartessos in southern Spain, but more recently as Tarshish in Sardinia. "Sheba" and "Seba" (v 10) are located respectively in modern Yemen is South Arabia and in an African nation (cf. Gen 10:7; Isa 43:3; 45:14).

The blessed future king and Messiah will invest himself on behalf of the "needy," the "afflicted," the "weak," and the "oppressed" along with those who are victims of "violence;" in other words, he will take up the cause of those who are destitute and cast aside by society at large (vv 12-14). Their lives ("blood" in v 14) are precious in the sight of that coming king. While King Solomon may have carried out some of these promises while he was king, it is clear, at least by the end of his reign, the ten northern tribes felt that Solomon had treated them badly, for they felt overtaxed and that they had been handled unfavorably in comparison with the tribe of Judah. It would be no surprise then, that Solomon's son, King Rehoboam, was unsuccessful in addressing the grievances against which Israel complained in the later years of Solomon's reign. Moreover, Solomon's reign never took in all the world's needy, poor, and oppressed; someone greater than Solomon was needed to finish the job. All this was work for the Messiah to come!

III. By Sensing How Prosperous and Blessed Messiah is to All – Ps 72:15-17

For a third time, the psalmist's prayer is enjoined for: (1) the unending perpetuation of the Davidic dynasty; (2) the security and economic thriving of the kingship; and (3) the extension of the king's great wealth in all areas of life. Once the conditions mentioned in verses 12-14 had been met, then the longevity of the just and righteous king could be described. This can be illustrated in the gifts that come from the subject nations, such as "gold from Sheba" (v 15; cf. 1 Kgs 10:14-15). Sheba, of course, is the land from which the queen of Sheba came to visit and test Solomon's wisdom (1 Kgs 10:1-13). It is located at the southwestern tip of the Arabian Peninsula in modern Yemen.

Even though God had given fruitfulness to the land of Israel during Solomon's day, still the prayer for the days of the coming of Messiah entailed a prayer that the land would be accompanied with an abundance of grain throughout the earth—that the stalks of grain would wave just as plentifully and beautifully as the trees of Lebanon, even from the most unexpected, but usually desolate places; namely, indeed even with the poorest growing conditions on the tops of the mountains (v 16). As A. A. Anderson put it:

> This verse (v 16) and the Psalm as a whole, shows that what we call the "moral realm" and the "realm of nature" form one indivisible whole to the Israelites. A community which lives according to righteousness enjoys not only the internal harmony, but also prosperity in field and flock.[38]

Some read "his name" instead of "his progeny" in verse 17. But this is not well supported by the text. The truth of an extensive "seed" is taught abundantly in other contexts (Isa 9:2; 49:20; Zech 2:8[4], but in this context it is the name of the Lord that is lifted high.

The use of the Hebrew Hithpael form of the verb *barak*, "to bless" (v 17b), is usually rendered reflexively, i.e., "bless themselves," as if all the nations of the world will see what is happening to Israel as they too will bless themselves! But this Hebrew form can be read just as well as a passive form of the verb, "will be blessed," as can be seen in two of the five instances where this verb appears in the same promise made in the Abrahamic Covenant (to Abraham: Gen 12:2-3; 18:18; 22:17-18; in the promise made to Isaac: Gen 26:3-4; and in the promise made to Jacob: Gen 28:13-14), which all use the Hebrew passive form of the verb in the same expression. To this day, most commentators remain skeptical about the passive meaning of the Hebrew Niphal stem (used in three of the five cases in the patriarchs), much less the Hebrew Hithpael (used in two of

38 A. A. Anderson. *The Book of Psalms*. 2 vols. New Century Bible Commentary (Grand Rapids: Eerdmans, 1972), 525.

the five cases). However, O. T. Allis's 1927 article presented strong evidence to the contrary, which has never been fully answered in its grammatical argument to this very day.[39]

Book II of the Psalms in which this Psalm itself ends with a doxology in verses 18-20, attributes to the Lord all the blessings that already have or will come from the reign of God's anointed one. The Lord is the worker of "marvelous deeds" or "wonders," a word that was also used of God's works in the plagues of Egypt against Pharaoh.

There is little wonder then that Isaac Watts (1674–1748) and James Montgomery (1771–1854) composed two hymns based on Psalm 72. Watts wrote:

Jesus shall reign where'er the sun
Does his successive journeys run:
His kingdom spread from shore to shore,
Till moons shall wax and wane no more.

People and realms of ev'ry tongue
Dwell on his love with sweetest song;
And infant voices shall proclaim
Their early blessings on his name.

Montgomery wrote "Hail to the Lord's Anointed:"

Hail to the Lord's Anointed.
Great David's greater Son!
Hail in the time appointed,
His reign on earth begun!
He comes to break oppression,
To set the captive free,
To take away transgression,
And rule in equity.

39 O. T. Allis, "The Blessing of Abraham," *Princeton Theological Review* 25 (1927):263-98. Also see Kaiser, *The Promise-Plan of God*, especially pp 17-67.

SUMMARY

The words of the psalmist are at one and the same time both a history of the past and a prophecy of what is to come. What they saw in a vision (*theoria*) held both the historical point of view in unity with the hyperbolic expressions that took them beyond the historical situation to the ultimate fulfillment of what is to come. David's line would finally produce a coming king who would rule with justice and righteousness as he defended the afflicted ones, the poor, and the needy in the last days. Under Messiah's rule and reign, peace, prosperity, and righteousness would be the order in that day. Indeed, all the kings of the earth would come to bow down before Messiah and to offer him their gifts as his rule endured forever, as long as the sun and moon endured.

CHAPTER 7

THE FREE GIFT OF SALVATION GIVEN BY MESSIAH

ISAIAH 55:1-13

Dr. Allan A. MacRae stated that "This [Isaiah passage] is one of the greatest Gospel calls to be found anywhere in the Scripture."[40] Derek Kidner agreed, as he too commented on this passage: "This call to the needy is unsurpassed for warmth of welcome even in the N.T."[41] It truly is one of the most gracious invitations to come free of charge to God's wonderful banquet of salvation, wherein everything has already been provided. Let us examine another great Messianic text.

Text: Isaiah 55:1-13

Title: "An Invitation to Salvation"

40 Allan A. MacRae, *The Gospel of Isaiah* (Chicago: Moody Press, 1977), 161.

41 Derek Kidner. "Isaiah," in *The New Bible Commentary: 21st Century Edition*, ed D. A. Carson Grand Rapids: Eerdmans, 1984), 629-70.

Homiletical Keyword and Interrogative: PROVISIONS. WHAT? (are the provisions that our Lord makes for his invitation to the salvation he offers?)

Teaching Aim: To show that the offer to enjoy personal salvation is a gift from the Lord who has provided everything that is needed for a full redemption.

Outline:

- ***I. The Gracious Invitation to Us All – 55:1-3a***
- ***II. The Gracious Host for All Who Attend– 55:3b-5***
- ***III. A Gracious Call to Repentance from All – 55:6-9***
- ***IV. A Gracious Word for All Our Hesitancies – 55:10-13***

Background:

I. The Gracious Invitation to Us All – 55:1-3a

The prophet, speaking on behalf of Yahweh, lifts his voice above its normal pitch as he tries to rally men and women from their generally sluggish response to God's invitations and shouts "Ho, hey hey!" That rendering may be a little too colloquial, but the Hebrew text does have the word Hoy, which is usually rendered by "Behold," or "Look here"—an attention-getting device. It is so difficult to arouse individuals, even when there is such a spectacularly free gift as is about to be offered here, that this audience, like all audiences, needs to be shaken up a bit by a loud call and some attention-getting devices, so that the audience's indifference is dropped, and the message is heard.

Some commentators hear, as the background for these verses suggest, the voice of a Near Eastern water vendor carrying a water pot on his back as he loudly hawks the water he has for sale. But the picture is more complicated than that, for there is also an invitation to receive grain, wine, and milk as part of a sumptuous fare that is available—all for no price and at no cost to the participant!

The only prerequisite is that those who "come" (a word used three times in verse 1 and one more time in verse 3a), only need to recognize that they are truly "thirsty." This is clearly a figurative expression, for it refers to more than a physical thirst for water, for even those who have an abundance of this world's goods and access to lots of water, exhibit a tremendous spiritual thirst for God and eternal things.

This invitation anticipated a similar teaching that Jesus would later give to the Samaritan woman in John 4:13-14. There Jesus taught the Samaritan woman, "Everyone who drinks this water will be thirsty again, but whosoever drinks the water I give him will never thirst. Indeed, the water I give will become in him a spring of water welling up to eternal life."

The people addressed here are not those restricted to Israel, but it is universal and open to anyone who is "thirsty." Even more startling is the fact that those who are invited to "come to the waters" (1b) are those "who have no money" (1c). They are also to "buy and eat.... without money and without cost" (1d, f). It appears, then, that those who are invited to this banquet are not only thirsty and hungry; they are also penniless and without the means to pay for such a feast.

Thus, the "water," "wine," and "milk," are figurative representations of all that is necessary for our spiritual life. Did not 1 Peter 2:2 later refer to the "sincere milk of the word" of God? As found in John 4:10, was not Christ himself the living water when he spoke to the Samaritan woman (John 4:10)? Thus, all are invited indiscriminately without respect to persons, or their ability to pay, or even without regard to their status. And would not Jesus later on shout out in the temple, "If anyone is thirsty, let him come to me and drink. Whoever believes in me, as the Scripture says, streams of living water will flow from within him." It surely seems as if our Lord were paraphrasing part of the same invitation Isaiah had given in Isaiah 55:1-3a. Therefore, only when we are utterly and spiritually destitute and have nothing in our impoverished souls to offer are we prepared to receive God's favor.

Still the question must be asked: "Why spend money on what is not bread and our labor on what does not satisfy?' (2a-b). This is nothing short of sheer madness and folly, for it is an outright rejection of God's kindnesses and graciousness. Therefore, our Lord condemns all methods by which men and women strive and contrive to obtain salvation in opposition to the free offer found in God's word. It is unconscionable to work our heads off for what is free, only to find that all that work brought no satisfaction and no promise of eternal life from God.

What folks really need to do is this: "Listen up folks, for I can tell you where you can get some good groceries that will really make your 'souls' delighted and satisfied." Bread alone will not do it; it will not assuage this type of hunger; nor will labor achieve it: it will come only by hearing the word of God and responding to that word of God by faith believing. This then, it must be stressed, is real "soul food," not the ordinary type of food that leaves one hungry shortly after we have eaten! It can only come from our LORD.

II. The Gracious Host to All Who Attend – 55:3b-5

The focus shifts now in verses 3b to 5 from the spiritual gifts that will be set in place at this banquet to the Host himself. Faith must have an object, and in both testaments, that object of faith must be placed in no one less that the coming Man of Promise, the Seed, the Lord Messiah himself.

The host for this banquet is the same one God had made "an everlasting covenant with," and given his faithful love to, namely: David" (3c-d). The Hebrew expression is most exact here, *hased dawid*, "[covenantal] love...to David," also translated as "mercies ... to David," or "kindnesses...to David." The Hebrew word *hesed* is one of the most beautiful words in that testament, for it occurs no less than 248 times and is almost without a single or even a multiple set of adequate English words to describe what God has done by freely offering his love and then maintaining it faithfully, despite the actions of those to whom he has given it. I would render this word simply as "grace." This expression, "the faithful love to David" only appears here in Isaiah 55:3d and in 2 Chronicles 6:42. But it is also noteworthy, because in Acts 13:34, the apostle Paul stated that the reason God raised up Jesus from the dead, never to decay, is because he promised, "I will give you the holy and sure blessings promised to David;"[42] surely the "grace [given] to David is intimately connected with the resurrection of Messiah.

The word rendered "sure," or "faithful" literally means that this promise given to David in 2 Samuel 7:15-16 is "made firm" and "definite." It is related to our word "Amen," with which we conclude our prayers. God had promised that the covenant he made with him would establish his house, which stood for his dynasty, and his kingdom forever. Never would God falter in his plan to carry this promise out to its conclusion. The promise made to David was a continuation of the same promise made in seminal form to Abraham, Isaac, and Jacob. All of these were affirmations of God's love and grace. In 2 Samuel 7:15, God promised: "my grace (*hasdi*) shall not depart from [David and his Seed], as I took it away from Saul, ... but your house and your kingdom will be made sure forever before you." The word for "sure" is the same one used in Isaiah 55:3d as the word translated as "faithful." This theme is echoed in many Old Testament passages.

Verses 4 and 5 each begin in the Hebrew text with a "Behold," or "See." In verse 4 David is to be a great "witness" to God's mercy to him and to all those who trusted in this coming Man of Promise from the line of his descent. But David was also a "leader" and a "commander of the peoples" (4b). What David was in a microcosmic way, his greater Son, our Lord Jesus, would be an even greater "witness," and the great "leader and commander" of all who would be redeemed through the work of the Lord's Servant described in the four Servant Songs in Isaiah.

Some want to transfer the promise from David to the whole nation of Israel based on verse 5. But to transfer the promise made to David and to give it over to the entire nation of Israel would run contrary to the emphatic claim that these promises made to David

---

42 See Walter C. Kaiser, Jr., "The Unfailing Kindnesses Promised to David: Isaiah 55:3," *JSOT* 45 (1989):91-98.

were "certain," or "unfailing," so that they would never depart from David or his line of descendants (2 Sam 7:15; Ps 89:37; as in Isa 55:3d).

David was startled by the divine announcement that he was the one who would receive a throne, a dynasty, and a kingdom (2 Sam 7:16), which would be "a charter for all humanity" (2 Sam 7:19, my translation)—meaning all the Gentiles as well as Israel. Thus, the principle of the offer of salvation to all nations was always in the promise-plan of God (Gen 12:3 c-d).

Accordingly, David was a "witness" to the truth of the gospel to the Gentiles, just as Jesus announced his purpose in his coming to be for the same purpose (John 18:37). Jesus would be that "second David" (Hos 3:5; Jer 30:9; Ezek 34:24). Likewise, the title "leader" (Hebrew *nagid*) is also expressly applied to Messiah (Dan 9:25; Acts 3:15; Heb 2:10; Rev 1:5). The title "commander" called attention to our Lord as the one who had the authority to give commandments or doctrine.

This section ends with a notice of the extent of the invitation: it would go out to all the nations. Note the plural number of the word "peoples" (a rather rare usage) and the two verbs: "they do not know you" and "they will hasten to you" (5b). This surely shows the efficacy of the call and the fact that it will be received (and has been received) by large numbers in the nations in a willing and jubilant way.

And if it be asked why there was such a great response among the nations or Gentiles, verse 5c-e explains it was "because of the LORD your God, the Holy One of Israel" (5c-d). Therefore, the power and the attractiveness did not rest in David, but in the Lord himself. Nations and Gentiles that never even heard of Israel will come, much like the promise in Isaiah 2:3, where people will come from all over the earth to hear the word of God taught in Zion/Jerusalem by Yeshua. Nevertheless, through the Servant, the Messiah, God has "endowed [Israel] with splendor" (5e). Zion's mountain has been made chief among the nations so that all nations can now stream to it to hear the Messiah teach them I that future day (Isa 2:2-4).

III. A Gracious Call to Repentance from All -55:6-9

The invitation to come to the Lord is amplified in verses 6-7. All are exhorted to "seek the LORD while he may be found; they must call on him while he is near. Let the wicked forsake his way and the evil man his thoughts. Let him turn to the LORD, and he will have mercy on him."

There are three new ideas that appear here. First, mortals are urged to seek God while he still may be found. The implication is that God will not always be available; it is a capital mistake to put off any decision about coming to the Lord on the pretense that there always will be another time or situation in which one could just as easily accept his offer. The Apostle Paul warned about this same type of procrastination. He said, "In the past God overlooked such ignorance [as that found among you Athenians], but now he commands all people everywhere to repent."

A second new idea that was not included in verses 1-2 was that it was required that the "wicked man forsake his [wicked] way and the evil [person] his [evil] thoughts" (7a-b). The order seems to be important, for God does not ask for some work of moral change in a person before he may drink of the water of life. But verses 6-7 make it clear that the one who accepts God's gracious invitation is expected to leave his or her wickedness and all evil thoughts. The point is this: no one can do this on their own strength, but the power to do so is found in what is taught in verses 1-2.

The third new note found in verses 6-7, but not announced in verses 1-2, is that God will "pardon" or "have mercy" on that one whose objective and subjective guilt for all their sins is removed and they are given a clean bill of health before God. God's "pardon" is wonderfully liberating in its cleansing effect.

Repentance is not an optional part of believing faith, for the human response to God's invitation is the need to "turn from one's sin" and to "turn to the Lord." The negative idea, to turn from sin is what we call "repentance," which includes a genuine and godly sorrow for our sin, or our making a "U-turn" away from the path we were traveling or headed on, and doing a 180 degree turning around to face the Savior, which is also turning to the gift of faith that comes from God.

We as mortals do not think like God thinks, neither are our ways similar to his ways (8a-b). The distance between us and God at this point is as great as the distance between heaven and earth. Accordingly, we must not start thinking that we cannot come to Christ now since we need to clean up our act and wait until we are looking like we are in much better shape. And we are warned, such ways of thinking are not the way God thinks, so why are we procrastinating? If the loving acts of a heavenly Father far outclass any pretense that we could make ourselves more attractive to the divine mercy, then why are we attempting to do the impossible? We were told in verses 1-2 that all this gift from God was without money and without cost, so we should stop thinking we can think and act like God can and does or that we can earn God's respect by what we pay him!.

Nothing troubles us more as humans than when we imagine God thinks and acts much as we act and think. Rather than taking his gracious offer, we often flee from him as if he were our enemy. Mortals, with corrupted hearts and minds, ought to shrink from daring to compare God's lofty nature with their own. God is not harsh and irreconcilable (an incorrect thought which only tends to harden mortals in their sin all the more); it is we who are more implacable and difficult to warm up to, after we have received an injury from someone else. Remember, God is nothing like any of us in such improper thinking!

IV. A Gracious Word for All Our Hesitancies – 55:10-13

To show the certainty and the full reliability of the promises of God, Isaiah gives us an analogy that depicts how rain and snow come down from heaven, but they do not come in vain, or for no purpose. Before that vapor returns back to the skies, it waters the earth, and then it makes things bud and flourish. That is precisely the way God's word operates: it "achieve[s] the purpose(s) for which [God] sent it" (11d).

God has not spoken in vain, nor has he scattered his promise-plan into thin air with little thought about what will happen as a result of his speaking. On the contrary, if the rain and the snow, also sent from God, can't and don't go back to heaven until they have done the job for which they were sent, who would dare to believe that God will let his promise, in the promise-plan of God, to Eve, Shem, Abraham, Isaac, Jacob and David fall inertly on the earth with little or no prospect of its coming to full fruition? That is as unthinkable as it is totally wrong. The word of God has an enormous force and power to bring about what is announced in that word. It remains one of the most powerful forces yet seen on planet Earth. So why do we think we are a special case, and the free offer of God's grace is not fully available to use? This is nothing more than disbelief of God and a trivializing of his word. One may as well give up the notion that the rain and snow have any good purpose on earth as to give up the effective force of that word in its free offer of salvation.

God will never allow his word to return to him "empty" and devoid of what he had intended it to accomplish (11b, d). It is simply not like human words, or those that come from fellow-human beings; these are the words of the infinite God. He will see that what he says does happen, for that is his nature and his way of acting. So, mortals should not fear that the word given to them about their salvation would fail or only be partially true.

Finally, the two last verses in this chapter present the great climax to God's work. These two verses introduce the results of the "pardon" God offers, and as such function as the conclusion of verses 6-13, as well as the argument of chapters 40–55.

As the people of Israel also met the conditions for repentance and accepted God's free offer of grace, the Lord also made possible their return to the land of Israel. Nature is poetically personified and is depicted as joyfully joining in Israel's joy and restoration. Metaphorically, the mountains and the hills celebrate with the Jewish people and the Gentiles in bursting forth in joyous song. Even the trees of the field start clapping their hands, a poetic reference if there ever was one (12 e-f).

The changes that will occur in the lives of those who come to know Christ are beautifully laid out in verse 13. The character and nature of these believers is as changed as if a "thorn bush" was replaced by a "pine tree" and "briers" were replaced with a "myrtle" tree (13 a-b).

All of this "will be for the LORD's renown" (13c). While there are strong figurative expressions in these two verses, that explanation hardly exhausts the total import of verses 12-13. As shown elsewhere in Scripture, one future day God will remove the curse that has been laid on the world since the Fall of Adam and Eve. He will bring the earth back to its original Edenic condition. There will be a regeneration of the land as Romans 8:22-25. This will all bring glory to God, as it points to God's eternal grace and power. What a great salvation!

SUMMARY

How aware are we of the deep spiritual hunger that exists all around us today? The table that the Lord sets will answer that hunger in every way. No price or cost to any of us mortals is associated with the free and gracious offer of salvation though so many want to take a shot at trying to earn their salvation when it is a free gift? The object of our saving faith is the Man of Promise, the Messiah, illustrated in the Servant of the Lord or Yeshua, who came in the line of David. Repentance is a necessary component of believing, for there must be a full turning to the Lord as we abandon the way and style of life we previously had.

CHAPTER 8

THE ATONEMENT OF MESSIAH THE SERVANT OF THE LORD

ISAIAH 52:13–53:12

It is not unusual for writers or readers of this fourth Servant Song in Isaiah 52:13–53:12 to remark in words similar to these: "without exaggeration, this text can be called the most important Scripture in the Old Testament." In fact, this text is frequently cited in the New Testament (e.g., in Luke 22:37; Acts 8:30-35; 1 Pet 2:22-25) as well as appearing in a number of Jewish and Christian writers down through the ages. Some have even conjectured that if we lost this passage in Isaiah from the Bible, we would be able to reconstruct most of it just from its citations in other sources. Perhaps one of the greatest commentators on this chapter, if not on the whole book of Isaiah, is by Franz Delitzsch, who claimed this was "the most central, the deepest, and the loftiest thing [found in] ... Old Testament prophecy, [nothing] outstripping it, has ever achieved."[43]

43 Franz Delitzsch, *Isaiah: Commentary on the Old Testament*. 2 vols. (Grand Rapids: Eerdmans, reprint 1973), 2:203.

Surely, this text is the informing theology that stands behind almost every portion in the New Testament that treats the events surrounding our Lord's passion, death, burial, resurrection, ascension, exaltation and second coming.[44] Its two-fold theme is nicely summarized in these words: it is about the sufferings and the glory of the Servant of the Lord.

Therefore, it is with added excitement that we turn to this marvelous text that has so wonderfully brought the importance, significance, and the triumphs of our Lord Jesus Christ to us in this Scripture.

Text: Isaiah 52:13–53:12

Title: "The Atoning Work of Messiah, the Servant of the LORD"

Focal Point: 53:6 "We all, like sheep, have gone astray, each of us has turned to his own way; and the LORD has laid on him, the iniquity of us all."

Homiletical Keyword and Interrogative: FEATURES. WHAT? (are the grand FEATURES of the Servant's death that have resulted in the atonement of those who believe in Yeshua?)

Teaching Aim: To examine as closely as possible exactly what it was that the Messiah did in his death on the cross and his resurrection for each and every one who believes,

Outline:

- ***I. The Startling Suffering and Success of the Servant – 52:13-15***
- ***II. The Superficial Estimate of the Servant's Rejection – 53:1-3***
- ***III. The Confession of the Servant's Vicarious Sufferings – 53:4-6***

44 Robert D. Culver, *The Sufferings and the Glory of the Lord's Righteous Servant* (Moline, IL: Christian Service Foundation, 1958), p. 20.

IV. The Unfair Treatment of the Servant in His Suffering, Death and Burial -53:7-9

V. The Plan, Satisfaction, and Exaltation of the Servant – 53:1-12

Background:

The distinctive nature of this fourth song is to be found in the details and purpose of Messiah's death and exaltation. And whereas in the other three songs[45] there was some disagreement on the extent of the songs, in this fourth song there is almost universal agreement that this fourth song extends form Isaiah 52:13 to 53:12. Most see five strophes of three verses each with Isaiah 52:13-15 acting as an introduction or a prologue and 53:10-12 as a conclusion or an epilogue. In both of these sections, it is fairly clear that it is Yahweh who is doing the speaking.

The intervening section of 53:1-3 is balanced off against 53: 7-9 with the center of this whole fourth song coming in the central section or strophe that comes in 53:4-6. Therein lies the great confession that served to give us the central teaching of the whole passage: "We all, like sheep, have gone astray... and the LORD has laid on him the iniquity of us all" (6a, c-d). That is why this passage gives us the greatest theological statement on the nature of the Atonement of Christ found anywhere in all of Scripture.

I. The Startling Suffering and Success of the Servant – 52:13-15

Right from the start of this fourth song, we are assured that the Servant, despite how things may appear as we proceed through the events narrated in the chapter that follows, "will have success" (13a). The Hebrew *yaskil,* is also rendered in English as "he will act wisely," or "he will prosper," but given its usage in Joshua 1:7-8, it seems best to rendering it as a prediction by the Lord of the success that the

45 The first Servant Song: Isaiah 42:1-9; the second Servant Song: Isaiah 49:1-7; and the third Servant Song: Isaiah 50:4-10.

Servant will enjoy, despite the agonies and the suffering he must go through to purchase our redemption.

This section also begins with a demonstrative particle, "Behold" or "See," which calls attention to the person and the fact of his success. Here is something that is startlingly new and wonderfully important, which also matches the way Isaiah 42:1 began in the first Servant Song, wherein the origin of the Servant was introduced. Thus, the two go together: the Servant's origin in Isaiah 42:1 and the culmination of his work in Isaiah 53:10-12.

What follows in the introduction in Isaiah 52:13b are three verbs of exaltation to describe the exceedingly high degree of success the Servant will enjoy. Whether these three verbs precisely point to three *stages* of the Servant's exaltation in: (1)his resurrection, (2) his ascension into heaven, and (3) his being seated at the right hand of the Father, cannot be determined with certainty. But what is certain is that he will end this ordeal with being "highly exalted" by God the Father and all who have benefited from his work on the cross.

Verse 14 introduces a comparison with the words "just as," which clearly forms the protasis (i.e., the clause expressing the condition, or the first part of a comparison). But the problem arises where the apodosis (i.e., the clause expressing the consequence of a condition, or the second part of the comparison) begins. The reason for the problem is because there are two clauses in Hebrew beginning with "so" (the first one is not translated in the NIV), which normally is the second half of the "Just as" clause. The two "so" clauses appear in 14b and 15a. But most correctly interpret the 14b clause to be an explanatory parenthesis, thereby leaving 15a clause to complete the comparison. Accordingly, "just as there were many who were appalled at him when they saw him crucified, ... So he will startle many nations" when kings see him come the second time in all his majesty and glory as King of kings and Lord of lords.

The reason so many were "appalled at him" is given in the parenthetical note that followed in verse 14b and c; "his appearance" and "his form" were both so shocking from the harsh experiences of the trial and his sufferings on the cross that they were stunned and could not believe he came from any sort of royalty or noble families, much less from heaven!

But over against that crowd of startled onlookers at his trial and at the site of his cross are the many stunned nations of verse 15a. These nations will likewise express amazement and surprise when they see such magnificence and such a display of power and authority as they have never seen before in their lives. But the Hebrew word *yazzeh*, is from the Hebrew verb, *nazah*, meaning "to sprinkle." But the Greek Septuagint in the third century BC rendered this verb into Greek meaning "to startle."[46] This meaning we adopt as fitting the context better (and even the parenthetical words that follow in 15b-d), where "kings will shut their mouths because of him. For what they have not heard, they will understand."

Of course, the objection to "sprinkle" cannot be that the Servant would not be given a priestly role, for he will be prophet, priest and king. But if "sprinkle" turns out to be the proper rendering, this fourth song does, in fact, refer to just that: the Servant's priestly role, but it does not do it as yet in this prologue. If the introduction does refer to this priestly function of "sprinkling," then the sprinkling of the nations would be understood as a spiritual cleansing of the nations in the Servant's atoning work.

However, despite the stunning effect that the suffering of the Servant will endure in his first coming (14) and the pure amazement that his second coming (15) will have on the kings of the earth, the Servant is assured of success in his work of atonement as we enter the body of this fourth song.

---

46 The Greek word used here is *thaumasontai*, meaning "to be astonished," or "show wonder." Most scholars in the past century followed the Greek understanding of this word, but recently there has been a trend back to "sprinkle."

II. The Superficial Estimate of the Servant's Rejection -53:1-3

The most difficult question to answer as we begin the main body of this fourth song is the identity of the speaker or speakers as we begin chapter 53. Three different answers have been given to this key question: (1) Some say it is the Gentile kings of 52:15, (2) others say, no, it is the prophet himself as a representative of all the prophets of Israel, or even as a representative of the nation Israel, or (3) it is the people of Israel, either as the returning exiles or of a future believing remnant, who are being addressed here.

As for the first option, the Gentile kings, they are too surprised about the Servant's exaltation, and they had not previously heard of such a person or happening. But those who now speak are those who have heard, but they simply would not believe. This may be why the apostle Paul quotes Isaiah 53:1 in Romans 10:16, as he complains against Israel's unbelief. Franz Delitzsch also helpfully adds: "whenever we find a 'we' introduced abruptly in the midst of a prophecy, it is always Israel that speaks."[47]

The double astonishment of Isaiah 52:13-15 now gives way to incredulity to those who have heard the report or "message" (53:1). The word "message" or "report" is a passive participle, meaning not "what we said," but "what we have heard." This would seem to have application to Israel, especially Israel of the end times (Zech 12:9-10). But the question is, "Who has believed [what we have heard]?" Putting the question this way seems to expect a negative answer; so we supply the answer: "few" have believed, or even "none" have!

A second rhetorical question is: "To whom has the arm of the LORD been revealed?" God's "arm" (cf. Isa 51:9; 52:10) speaks of his power to save in this case, so how many have experienced this power to save? Again, very few, if any! Thus, there has been a clear rejection of the Servant's words/message and his long-standing promise-plan that began in Genesis 3:15 and continued on in Genesis 9:27; 12:2-3; 49:10; 2 Samuel 7:14-19. And if that was not enough, the

---

47 Delitzsch. *Isaiah* 2:310.

Servant's deeds, works and evidences of his power to deliver in the past have also been disregarded. Jesus had taught in John 12:37-40, after he had done many miracles in their midst, yet they too did not believe him, he said this was happening so that Isaiah 53:1 might be fulfilled.

Not only were his message and deeds rejected; he himself was rejected in his own person. First, they depicted the lowly beginning of his life's career. They saw no regal splendor or military power to rid them from the clutches of Roman dominion; no, they compared him to a stunted plant that was like a tender shoot that grew up out of the main stalk as a shoot, or like a root out of dry ground. He was too back-woodsy and too rustic for anyone to waste their time on. He exhibited none of the marks of beauty or majesty that would make us want to desire him.

Five sad statements in verse 3, then, describe the full nature of his rejection. First, he was "despised," which Robert D. Culver explained is "the most comprehensive of all the terms here [used twice in this verse], involving that complete act of the whole man when he utterly and completely refuses something."[48] Secondly, he was "rejected by men," or even "shunned by men." Thirdly, he was a "man of sorrows and familiar with suffering," referred to his suffering on the cross, wherein he experienced pains and aches of all kinds, both physical and mental. Fourthly, he was "Like one from whom men hide their faces," and we want to have nothing to do with that type of person. Finally, and worst of all, "he was despised [Isaiah repeats this verb] and we esteemed him not." As we mortals viewed the scene at the cross, we decided that he was of no account and it all added up to us as one big zero. The Servant's rejection could not have been more complete nor could he have been more totally devalued than he was in this account of his death.

48 Culver. *The Sufferings and the Glory*, 53.

III. The Confession of the Servant's Vicarious Atonement – 53:4-6

These three verses in this third strophe of the Fourth Servant Song describe the substitutionary death of the Servant. Ten times Isaiah used the first-person pronoun, "us," "we," or "our" in these three verses to show that Christ's suffering was "for us."

Verse 4 describes the human occasion of Christ's suffering: "He took our infirmities." The Servant took the full weight of the guilt and the consequences of our sin. Several items strongly support the substitutionary aspects of the atonement, even though there have been many attempts to deny it, or to dilute it. Note the close parallels with the Day of Atonement in Leviticus 16, where some count as many as eleven phrases that show verbal similarities of substitution between this text and Leviticus 16.[49] Moreover, verse 10 later on will identify the Servant's death as a "Guilt Offering."

If verse 4 gives us the human occasion for the atonement, then verse 5 gives us the divine act that took place in the atonement. Note the passive form of the verbs in this verse in which God is emphatically the actor. There are four expressions of what God did to the Servant: (1) "He was pierced" by the nails in his hands and his feet along with the sword in his side; (2) "He was crushed/ bruised" by the slap on the face and the cross-dragging; (3) the punishment ...was upon him," which answered to what we today would call the gallows, the electric chair, the firing squad or the lethal injection, and (4) "by his wounds we are healed," which points to Pilate having Jesus scourged and the soldiers smiting him with their reeds. But all of this was for "our transgressions," "for our iniquities," for "our peace," and for our "heal[ing]."

The great confession comes in verse 6. We all have acted like sheep, for that is the herd instinct that speaks to our depravity. We are sinners by nature with an inborn tendency towards sin since

49 W. Kay. "Isaiah: Introduction, Commentary and Critical Notes," in *The Bible Commentary*, ed. F. C. Cook, vol 5 (Grand Rapids: Baker, 1981), 266.

Adam and Eve fell. But there is more: "each of us has turned to his own way" (6b), for we are also sinners by choice as well. But Messiah bore both our depravity and our personal sin in his own body on the tree. As such, "God was in Christ reconciling the world" (2 Cor 5:19).

IV. The Unfair Treatment of the Servant in His Suffering, Death, and Burial -53:7-9

In this stanza, we are told how the Servant will suffer, die, and be buried. Each verse picked up one of these three treatments of the Servant. Thus, in verse 7, it describes how he was oppressed, much as Israel was at the hands of her Egyptian slave-masters (Exod 5:6), but the Servant offered no resistance to his tormentors. "He was led like a lamb to the slaughter and as a sheep before her shearers is silent, so he did not open his mouth" (7c-e). The Servant is likened to the silence of the sheep at the time of their sheering. Never has anyone ever heard a bleating sound from a sheep as it was being sheared despite the rough treatment it may receive from new or inexperienced shearers. In like manner, Jesus refused to answer the chief priests, Pilate, and Herod, for he too was silent before his accusers and soldiers (Matt 27:12-14; Luke 23:9).

Verse 8 predicted the circumstances of his death. The scene of his death is remarkable for the way it contravened every legal and civil aspect of the law. Truly it was "By oppression and judgment he was taken away." This translation is too tame here, for it is better rendered that he "was snatched away," or "hurried away." The arrest of Jesus in the Garden on that night and the judicial proceedings of the next day moved so swiftly that it boggles the mind at the injustice of it all. There were five speedy trials, all illegal: first by Annas (John 18:13), then at the High Priest's palace before the Sanhedrin (Matt 26:57-66), then on to Pilate (Matt 27:1-2), and yet another questioning before Herod (Luke 23:11-26), and then came the final judgment (Matt 27:1-2). But the heartbreak of it all was this: "Who can speak of his descendants?" (8b). Or, to put it more colloquially, "Who gave a hoot?" Did anyone of his contemporaries consider it? Who was going to speak up on his behalf? No one spoke up in his defense!

The Servant "was cut off from the land of the living: for the transgression of my people was he stricken" (8c-d). Jewish scholars at the beginning of the Christian era strongly emphasized the fact that the "he" at the end of verse 8 is usually translated elsewhere as a plural, so they felt it was the nation Israel that was sufferings here, and not an individual Servant who was bearing the sin of the world, much less their sin! But there are clear examples in Hebrew grammar where the Hebrew *lemo*, "to him/them," is rendered as a singular "he" or "him" (Gen 9:26 and Isa 44:15), so there is no need to translate it as Jewish apologists did: "For the sin of my people were they stricken."

If this clause did point to Israel, why is this passage never read in the synagogues even to this day, when this text could have given comfort to millions of Jewish people, even when the passages all around Isaiah 53 are read rather routinely in Jewish synagogues?

The ninth verse went on to talk about his burial. The Servant "was assigned a grave with the wicked [ones]," for the word for "wicked" is in the plural number, and thus it predicted that our Lord would be crucified between two thieves. But even more astonishing is the fact that verse 9b proceeded to say that the Servant would be assigned "a grave with the rich," wherein the word for "rich" was in the singular form, allowing this to be fulfilled in the request Joseph of Arimathea, a secret disciple of Jesus (Matt 27:57-60). All of this happened, yet Isaiah comments: "though he had done no violence, nor was any deceit in his mouth" (9c-d). Neither one of these statements could have been made of anyone in Israel, for the prophet had described the nation from the beginning of his prophecy to be a "sinful nation, as people loaded with guilt" (Isa 1:4a, b). Only the Servant could fit this description.

V. The Plan, Satisfaction and Exaltation of the Servant – 53:10-12

The success of the Lord's plan is seen first in the fact that the Servant's suffering and sacrificial death were entirely within the plan and will of the Lord. None of this could have happened without God authorizing it and planning it, for "it was the LORD's will to crush him and cause him to suffer" (10a-b). Christ's death was not an accident. Mortals could meanly carry out the jealousies of their anger, but only the Lord could make the Servant's life "a guilt offering" for the sin of all (10c; cf. 1 Pet 1:20; Acts 2:23). A "guilt offering" emphasizes the expiatory nature of the death of Christ, for as one of the main Levitical sacrifices (Lev 5:14-6, 7; 7:1-6). The sacrifice discharged the debt owed and set the person free, for the compensation had been paid in full. While the Jewish people were guilty and culpable for their acts of false arrest and illegal trials, not to mention their guilt for his crucifixion, but even this act must also be attributed to the permissive will of God (cf. Acts 2:23; 4:28).

Five divine results came from the Servant's suffering and death on the cross, all of which are evidence of the huge success of the plan and will of God. The first result is that "He will see his seed/ offspring" (10c). This agrees with Psalm 22:30 where a "seed/ posterity will serve him." It also agrees with Hebrews 2:10, where he will "bring...many sons to glory." This is the "seed" that had also been promised to Abraham and David as well.

The second evidence of his success is that he will "prolong his days" (10c). This did not refer to the usual length of days lived, but it was the reward for those who had passed through death and were among those over whom "death had no more dominion" (Isa 9:6-7), or as in Revelation 1:18, where Yeshua declared, "I was dead and behold I am alive forever and ever."

The third result is that "The will/plan of the LORD will prosper in his hands" (10d). What Isaiah had outlined in the first and second Servant Songs (Isa 42; 49), would now be accomplished. The Servant would be the mediator of the New Covenant and he would bring righteousness to the nations as well as he would bring Jacob back to her land and be a light to the Gentiles, and give salvation to the ends of the earth. What an enormous "hand" and work, in all that needed to be done, was seen in the work of the Servant!

The fourth result was that "he would see the light of life and be satisfied" as a result of all his labor and travail (11a). What the Servant saw was a world filled with the knowledge of God as the waters cover the sea (Isa 11:9; Hab 2:14). He could also see a glorious Church without spot or wrinkle (Eph 5:27) and he could see a new heaven and a new earth (Isa 65–66).

The final and fifth result is more difficult to render: "By his knowledge, my righteous Servant will justify many" (11c). The solution here may be in a cognate Ugaritic word that is spelled much as "knowledge" is spelled in Hebrew, but that word means "sweat." That would make sense here, for it would be "by his sweat many would be justified."

This last stanza of the cycle of five strophes in 52:13–53:12 mentions two gifts in verse 12: "I will give him a portion among the great," and "he will divide the spoils with the strong." Revelation 19:14 had promised the spoils of the coming world-wide victory would be shared with the saints. This is similar to Psalm 110:3.

This whole passage concludes with four divine reasons why God's seal of approval would be put on his Servant/Messiah: (1) "Because he poured out his life unto death" (12c), (2) Because he allowed himself to be "numbered with the transgressors" (12d), (3) Because "He bore the sin of many" (12e), and (4) Because he "made intercession for the transgressors" (12 f).

The Servant was more than worthy of any and all compensation that was now offered to him, for the salvation he had accomplished was the greatest gift ever given to mortals on planet earth.

SUMMARY

Isaiah 52:13-15 begins this fourth Servant Song by assuring us all that the Messiah will have success despite his brutal suffering and agony on the cross. The second stanza of this song in Isaiah 53:1-3 shows how superficial most regarded Messiah's death while the heart of this chapter is Isaiah 53:4-6 where all who trust in Messiah confess that "All we like sheep have gone astray and turned each to his or her own way." The fourth stanza in verses 7-9 show how unfair Messiah's treatment on the cross was both in his death and his burial and the song concludes in verses 10-12 by announcing Messiah's plan for the future and his exaltation in what has been accomplished for all sinners.

CHAPTER 9

THE MESSIAH THE RESTORER OF DAVID'S COLLAPSING DYNASTY

AMOS 9:11-15

The Scofield Reference Bible stated that "dispensationally, this [text of Acts 15:13-18, which quotes Amos 9:11-12], is the most important passage in the NT."[50] It went on in that same context to argue: "The verses that follow in Amos describe the final ingathering of Israel, which the other prophets invariably connect with the fulfillment of the Davidic Covenant."

On the other hand, O. T. Allis, the late, titular Dean of Evangelical Old Testament professors (if I might make such a new appointment and title), in the early twentieth, announced a somewhat different conclusion about this passage. Allis taught, "That James [in Acts 15] declares expressly that Peter's experience at Caesarea, which he speaks of as God's visiting 'the Gentiles to take out of them a people for his name,' was in accord with the burden of prophecy as a whole

50 *Scofield Reference Bible*, p. 1343, however when this same reference tool stated on p. 1169 what were the pivotal chapters in prophecy as a whole, this text was not included, but Deut 28, 29, 30, Ps 2, and Dan 2 and 7 were mentioned instead.

and quotes freely from Amos in proof of it."[51]

So, which of these two analyses is correct? Were both interpretations of Acts 15 presenting equally correct interpretations about the meaning of this prophecy, while taking opposite points of view, or was one interpreter incorrect, or were both of their interpretations wrong? Accordingly, one interpretation seemed to stress an exclusive Judean nationalistic sense of the similar words found in the Davidic Covenant for a future rule and reign of Israel with its promise of a kingdom, a throne and a dynasty for David and a restored nation of Israel, while the other interpreter gave pretty much a solely spiritual interpretation that focused on the expansion of the Gentiles and the blessing that was to come on the New Testament Church. Could both be correct? How could that be when so when the authoritative meaning intended by the prophet Amos seemed to be clear? And what about the meaning of this text posed by James, the leader of the early Church? And could we still say that the Old and New Testaments were in agreement on the meaning of this text, or was there a dual meaning that could be assigned to the same text? These are the questions that this text presents to us. To learn what is the best answer that can be given to these questions, we need to go to the text itself!

THE "COLLAPSING HUT/BOOTH" OF DAVID – AMOS 9:11A

Amos had previously just completed the section of his prophecy dealing with the five visions that were communicated to him in Amos 7–9, each of which began with the introductory formula: "Thus the LORD Yahweh showed me" (7:1, 4, 7; 8:1; 9:1), but the paragraph that begins with 9:11, however, did not claim that it too was a vision. To be sure, there are items in 9:11 and the following verses that repeat some aspects of the topics raised in the previous five visions

51 O. T. Allis, *Prophecy and the Church* (Philadelphia: Presbyterian and Reformed, 1945), 147.

concerning the future of Israel and God's future kingdom reign, but the prophet Amos had majored, on the theme of the judgment that would fall, particularly on Israel for its sin. Despite its emphasis on judgment, Amos interspersed occasional concepts of a future hope for Israel and the nations of the world. For example, Amos 5:14 held out the promise of the presence of the LORD, just as Amos 5:18-20 likewise focused on the coming final and great Day of the LORD. In fact, there were a good number of promises that were attached to "that [coming] day" in 3:14; 4:2; 8:3, 9, 11, 13, as distinguished from some of the prophet's previous contemporary emphases, which dwelt on the blackness of the night and certainty of death and God's judgment for the sin of the people. Therefore, we can affirm that the theme of a future hope was not completely missing from Amos's earlier words, so we should not think it strange that a concept of a future hope would also be found in this text of Amos 9:11-15, as some scholars have needlessly rejected.

The "day of Yahweh," as a matter of fact, looked forward to a time when God would establish his future kingdom. Some have argued that the origins of that "day of the LORD" had originated in the pagan celebration in the Near East of the secular "New Year's festival," in which the ruler of the nation was annually again recognized as king and his covenant as king was renewed for the coming new year. But there is scant evidence, if any at all, for such a syncretistic joining of a pagan festival with the Biblical theology of the "Day of Yahweh." They did not appear to share a common heritage at all.

As for the Amos text in 9:11-15, he began by focusing on the "falling/collapsing hut/booth of David," whose present dilapidated condition as David's *sukka*, i.e., his "hut," or "booth," (now less than a "house") was the subject of the good news the prophet Amos needed to announce. What had previously been called David's "house" (*bayit david*) was now being described as a former "house" that had been reduced to a "collapsing/falling-down booth/hut." The royal "house/dynasty" of David (2 Sam 7:5, 11), had fallen now into its current decrepit and run-down condition, so that by now it could be viewed as being in a deplorable, broken-down and collapsing structure or dynasty that was in an urgent and needful state of disrepair—David's "house" was now described as a "falling/collapsing booth/hut."

Nevertheless, note that Amos's prophecy was set for a future divine rectification of this condition, for "in that day" a total fulfillment of God's ancient promise to David and his "house" would occur at the time of the second coming of our Lord (9:11a). It would not remain in such a deplorable condition, but the Lord himself would raise up that "hut" once again to be the "house/dynasty of David."

What followed in this context, we must carefully observe, were three important verbs, each of which had the first-person suffixial pronoun attached to each of the three verbs; these designated what would one day come to pass, with some of its noted features, such as our Lord had already promised would happen long ago. Our Lord himself declared (by the four "I will" statements included in this text) that he would perform the work of raising up and repairing the dilapidated "tent/hut of David" as the task of restoring it to its former status as a "house," or the royal dynasty that God intended it to be. Indeed, it would be nothing less than the celebrated "dynasty" of David once again! This reference to a "booth of David," or a "hut," is an obvious substitute for the majestic pre-Solomonic term, pointing to the "House of David" (2 Sam 7:11). David's "house" (i.e., what pertains to his throne, dynasty, and kingly line of descendants) had now become, in the interim in the prophet Amos's day, reduced to little more than a "crumbling [or: broken down] hut," even a "falling-down booth," that was nothing more than a pile of branches arranged on a simple framework structure, such as was used by Israel during her days of wandering in the wilderness or during the annual celebration of the feast of booths. Considering this sad and decrepit state of collapse, the Lord had now stepped in and promised that that awful state would now cease, for he would rectify that poor state by the very work of his own hands in that coming "Day of the LORD". The text read this way:

"I will raise up the fallen booth of David,
I will repair (its) [feminine plural pronoun: "their"] breaches/ broken walls;
I will raise up (its) [masculine singular pronoun: "his"] ruins,
I will build (it) [feminine singular pronoun: "her"] as in the days of old." (Amos 9:11).

The Hebrew present participle used here (of the "falling/ collapsing" booth) emphasized, the impending state of its near collapse and in need of immediate repair. Accordingly, the "dynasty/ house of David," our Lord taught through the prophet Amos, would temporarily suffer shame and reproach, but he also promised that our LORD would raise it from its collapsing situation to a fully restored condition, for he had promised with his own word that he would complete raising that house of David up again in that grand future "day of the LORD." On such a repair of that "house/booth of David" hung the very promises God had made in earlier covenant, which had announced David's future rule and reign of the kingdom of God in 2 Samuel 7 and 1 Chronicles 17!

GOD'S RESTORATIVE WORK ON THE DAVID'S DISHEVELLED HUT – AMOS 9:11B-D

Most interpreters (and translators) fail to notice the distinctive personal pronoun suffixes on the words that follow in Amos 9:11b, c, and d, which we have already briefly referred to above. The theology of this passage will be mightily affected by a correct understanding of each of these suffixes, as can also be seen from the agreeable context that follows verses 11-12!

C. F. Keil is certain that "the plural suffix ('breaches *thereof*,' pirsehem) can only be explained from the fact that the sukkah, "booth," actually refers to the present condition or state of the kingdom of God, which in Israel was by this time divided into two kingdoms ("these kingdoms," ch. vi. 2)."[52] In other words, God would repair and wall-up the rent and the separation and division that had come between the two southern tribes of Judah and Benjamin with the ten northern tribes of Israel, who had bolted from the unified nation of Israel in 931 BC. For ever since then, under the rebellious leadership of Jeroboam I, no longer had Israel been one nation, but they had been divided into two nations. But now Amos promised that the Lord would heal "<u>their</u> breaches" [i.e., the division that had come between them]! Thus, this note of a future reunification of the separated nations back into one unified nation would be sounded again in the sixth century by the prophet Ezekiel, who also clearly predicted the future union of the ten northern tribes of Israel with the two southern tribes of Judah and Benjamin in Ezekiel 37:15-28, where he symbolically put the two sticks together to form one nation. But Amos, in the eighth century BC, had already anticipated this reunification by his prediction for a long time prior to Ezekiel's sixth century promise, thus Amos was not alone in preaching this future action of reunification of the two nations into one unified people once again by our Lord.

The second suffix attached to a noun, which surely was a masculine suffix, ("his ruins," *harisotayw*) must refer to no one other than to David himself, and not to the "hut," which would require a feminine pronoun as the appropriate matching antecedent. Even if it had been antecedent to the word "breaches," it too would likewise require a feminine plural pronoun. Consequently, under the new coming of David (as the Messiah) the dilapidated hut of David would be raised from the ashes of collapse and disrepair to provide for God's sovereign rule and reign over the entire globe in that day of the Lord.

Accordingly, what had affected the nation of Israel, had also had an impact on the Davidic person himself. Thus, when these first two

---

52 C. F. Keil, *Biblical Commentary on the Old Testament: Minor Prophets* (Grand Rapids: Eerdmans, 1954), I:330.

acts of correctly identifying the attached pronouns have been noticed, then a third clause with a third pronominal suffix of "rebuilding her" (*benitiha*) must claim our attention. It could be identified as referring to the temple, as C. F. Keil contended, for *banah* in this connection meant "to finish building, to carry on, enlarge, and beautify the building."[53] However, the feminine singular pronominal suffix used here could better refer, of course, to the "falling hut/booth" itself. But it is also worth noting, especially in light of the important phrase that completes this clause, "as it was in days of old," for this clause is one of the keys to this passage. It clearly pointed back to the promise contained in 2 Samuel 7:11, 12, 16, where God promised he would raise up David's seed after him, and give to him a "throne, dynasty/ house, and kingdom" that would endure "forever." Now in Amos, the resurrecting of David's dilapidated "booth" would involve raising up a kingdom, a seed, and a dynasty. In fact, verse 12 added "in order that they might inherit the remnant,' which in this case clearly was the people of God in Israel. The restoration of the Jewish people to their Messiah clearly was a part of God's plan for the coming kingdom and reign of God!

Therefore, what is decisively taught here is this: "David" and his "house," i.e., his dynasty and his Jewish people, called here the "remnant," are indissolubly linked together as part of the total picture of what God would do "in that day," especially as it related to his kingdom rule and reign.

THE REMNANT OF EDOM AND ALL THE NATIONS – AMOS 9:12

Amos's reference to "the remnant of Edom," however, appear to some interpreters to be a most troublesome insertion in this prophecy. Nevertheless, this allusion to "Edom" should not be viewed in a negative, retaliatory, or even in an interruptive manner, as if it meant

53 Keil, *Minor Prophets*, p 330.

that there was a punishment to be visited on Edom as one of Israel's rivals. On the contrary, this time the prophecy about "Edom" in Amos was meant to show that this nation, perhaps as representative of the other nations in this world, would be brought under that coming rule and reign of David, who was soon to appear as none-other than king Messiah. This nation of Edom would be part of the larger remnant of the Gentiles, who would also share in the covenant promises made to King David.

It was no one less that the late Gerhard Hasel who demonstrated that the word "remnant" was used in Amos in a threefold manner: (1) "to refute the popular remnant expectation which claimed all of Israel was to be the [redeemed] remnant" (Amos 3:12; 4:1-3; 5:3; 6:9-10; 9:1-4). Over against this view, with its bleak descriptions of doom, or one with little hope for Israel, there was predicted in the concept of the "remnant," which would be at the very least a core of the redeemed; (2) "to show there will indeed be a "remnant" *from* Israel" (Amos 5:4-6, 15) in that great future day located in eschatological time; and (3) "to include also the 'remnant of Edom,' along with the neighboring nations, who also would be recipients of the outstanding promises in the Davidic tradition" (Amos 9:12).[54]

Amos singled out the nation of Edom because of their persistent hostility to the people of God, similar to the role that the Amalekites had played in the earlier days of Israel (Exod 17:8ff; Deut 25:17-19), and who likewise opposed the kingdom of God most violently.

But even beyond these background statements, Edom's representative role was stressed in the ep-exegetical note that appeared in verse 12—"and/even all the nations/Gentiles who are called by my name." Therefore, the point of this passage is not about Edom coming under Israel's military subjugation and conquest; instead, it is best understood to mean that Edom's spiritual incorporation in the people of God was possible, along with the other Gentiles to form an enlarged kingdom of David, as the view that the prophet

54 Gerhard Hasel, *The Remnant* (Berrien Springs, MI: Andrews University, 1972), 393-94

had in mind here! For, just as the ancient promise of God had been made to Abraham that the people of Israel would act as the channel for "all the families of the earth to be blessed by Abraham and his seed," so this passage agreed with that point of view, as it made the same point (Gen 12:3).

But was this reading of the Hebrew text the most accurate textual reading, or had the translators of Amos 9:11-12 failed to detect a few important nuances?

WHICH TRANSLATION IS CORRECT? "POSSESSION OF THE REMNANT OF EDOM" OR "IN ORDER THAT THE REST OF MANKIND MAY SEEK THE LORD?" – AMOS 9:12

The result of our Lord's restoring the kingdom of Israel and his raising up the dilapidated booth of David would be that Israel's military and political power would first of all be that the territory that God had originally promised to Israel would be given back to them. The Hebrew text of verse 12 is a linguistic continuation of verse 11. To be sure, if the verb "to take possession of" (*yirshu*) was the original reading in Amos 9:12, then it was chosen by Amos because of an earlier statement in Balaam's prophecy of Numbers 24:17-18. There Balaam had predicted that a "star" and a "scepter" (i.e., symbols for the Messiah) would arise in Israel "to take possession (*yerasha*) of Edom .... while Israel [nevertheless] did valiantly." Accordingly, the Man of Promise, i.e., the Messiah, would arise from within Israel and he would exercise dominion over the nations, prophesied Balaam, for his kingdom would spread over all the earthly kingdoms, such as Moab, Sheth, Edom, Amalek, and Asshur. God would take from these middle eastern nations, and here particularly the representative nation of Edom, a territory belonging to his own possession as he simultaneously extracted a believing "remnant" from all the nations of the world, including, as we note again now in the Amos passage, some of those who were like what usually were similar to the hostile nation of Edom.

However, if the recently discovered alternative text from the Dead Sea Scrolls found in the Qumran collection of texts, whose reading in Amos 9:12 (4Q174) is the preferred textual reading, then, according to this Qumran text, Amos did not refer in his book to the Lord's "possessing Edom," but instead that text referred to a "seeking of the Lord by a remnant of humanity." Thus, the object of the verb "to possess" in the MT has now become the subject of this phrase, and the rendering of the phrase the "remnant of Edom" has become "the remnant of humanity," in which *'edom* is now read as *'adam,* meaning "humanity" or "mankind" (because the consonants are identical in Hebrew), then this is how these two different readings could have come about as well as which one is very plain sense once one views the ancient form of the Hebrew text. For, instead of reading Hebrew yod, which began the Hebrew word for "possessing," and which rendered the root *yrsh,* "to possess," we read instead an initial *dalet,* giving the root *drsh,* "to seek," then the Qumran reading and the reading in Acts begins to make sense. Again, note that the difference in the orthography in the Hebrew script of that time was indeed very small, for it was only the length of the downstroke of the pre-Masoretic Hebrew letter *yod* that made the difference between the *yod* and the *daleth*! In that case, verse 12 would now read: "in order that the remnant of humanity may seek the Lord, even all the nations/Gentiles that are called by my name." In fact, that is exactly how James quoted this verse in Acts 15:16-17. Both points about Messiah's future work are made in Scripture, of course, but the DSS reading seems to be the authoritative rendering of Amos since the next phrase that follows this reading about the "remnant of humanity" is "even/and all the nations that are called by my name" (9:12b). Moreover, that is how the Septuagint also read this text in Amos. Likewise, the New Testament reading in Acts 15:16-17 agreed with the DSS word to "seek," (*darash*) instead of the Masoretic rendering of "possess" (*yarash*). Thus, we now have a Hebrew reading for Amos that agrees with the New Testament rendering of Amos, both making the same point.

Accordingly, there was a real hope in Amos for the coming Messiah beyond the present disaster of the fall of Samaria in 721 BC. Amos concluded his prophecy in 9:11-15 by promising that God would rebuild David's house/dynasty, which at the moment that Amos spoke, was currently in a dilapidated condition, one which could only be likened to a "collapsed hut" or "fallen booth of David" (*sukkah David hannophelet*). Thus, what normally, under better circumstances, would have been styled "the house (*bet*) of David" (2 Sam 7:5, 11; 1 Kgs 11:38; Isa 7:2, 13), i.e., David's dynasty, was at that time until the coming future, in a tragic state of disrepair with "breaches" or "ruins" around it. The Hebrew active participle (*hannophelet*) stressed either its present state of collapsing, or that it was proceeding to be in the process of "falling" into ruin, and about to fall down. Thus, the dynasty of David would suffer, but thanks be to God, he would bring it back from its deterioration, for God himself had promised that this house of David was an eternal house.

Under a new, but coming David, Messiah himself declared that he would rebuild David's dynasty "as it was in the days of old," a phrase that clearly pointed back to the antecedent theology of 2 Samuel 7:11-12, 16. Moreover, the pronouncement of 2 Samuel 7:19, where David was sure that <u>what</u> God had given to him in the Davidic Covenant was nothing less than "a charter/law /instruction for all humanity" (*torat ha'adam*). Amos seems to repeat the substance of that same promise in Amos 9:12 by saying: "in order that the remnant of humanity (*she'erit 'adam*) may seek the Lord, even all the nations that are called by my name."[55]

55 For further elaboration, see Walter C. Kaiser, Jr., "The Davidic Promise and the Inclusion of the Gentiles (Amos 9:11-15 and Acts 15:13-18: A Test Passage for Theological Systems," *JETS* 20 (1977): 97-111.

The usage of the phrase "called by my name" in the Old Testament always placed each of the objects so designated under divine ownership. What God named, he thereby owned and ruled over, whether it was a city (2 Sam 12:28; Jer 25:29; Dan 9:18-19), or a man or a woman (Isa 4:1; Jer 14:9; 15:16; 2 Chron 7:14). Thus, when Israel walked by faith, Moses promised "All the peoples of the earth shall see that you are called by the name of the LORD" (Deut 28:10). But when they refused to believe, they were "like those who [were] not called by your [God's] name" (Isa 63:19). This phrase is very much like Joel 2:32 [Heb. 3:5]; "All who call upon the name of the LORD."[56]

SUMMARY

Two images of agricultural blessing are given in Amos 9:13—(1) the reaper (*qotser*) will be overtaken by the one plowing (*horesh*) the ground, and (2) the one sowing seed (*moshek hazara'*) would overlap the one treading grapes. These agricultural hyperboles mentioned here emphasize the enormous bounty that the anticipated harvest would produce, so that the farmers of that day would hardly be finished one aspect of harvesting the crops from the previous season, when the time for sowing the next season's crops would have overtaken them. Accordingly, the promise was that the time was coming when the earth would be so fertile and so abundant in its production that there would be no time elapsing between harvesting from one season's super abundance of crops and the season for planting of the seed for the next season! Thus, the enormity of the grape harvest would be so plentiful, to use another hyperbole, that it would be as though the mountains and hills on which the vineyards were planted were now dripping and flowing over the hillsides with new wine (13b). Israel would be up to their necks, so to speak, with

56 For a full study of this phrase and concept, see Walter C. Kaiser, Jr., "Name," in *Zondervan Pictorial Encyclopedia of the Bible*, ed. M. C. Tenney (Grand Rapids: Zondervan, 1975), 4:360-70.

grape juice and wine!

This message from God ends with the fulfillment of the restoration promised in Deuteronomy 30:3-5, when Israel would return to the land of Canaan to repossess their ancient land (14a). In that future day, Israel will rebuild her ruined cities in a land that apparently will have been previously razed by war. Israel will live in their cities once again. They will plant vineyards and drink its wine. They will work the fields and eat from their produce. The blessing of God will be poured out on them as never before!

Just as Israel will plant gardens, so God will replant the people of Israel in their own land once more, but what is different about this time is that Israel will never again be later uprooted and dispossessed out of the land God had originally given to them (15b-c). There would be no more exiles taken from Israel into foreign countries and no more serving as captives to foreign governments. Israel would once more be at home, never to be dispossessed of the gift that had been given to his people in this land.

CHAPTER 10

THE PLACING OF THE CROWN ON THE HEAD OF THE MESSIAH – THE ONE TO WHOM IT RIGHTFULLY BELONGS

EZEKIEL 21:18-27

The prophet Jeremiah had been preaching approximately thirty years in Jerusalem when another prophet named Ezekiel was carried off into foreign captivity with the other exiles in 597 BC to Babylon, which was eleven years before the Fall of Jerusalem in 586 BC. Prior to that event, Daniel and his three friends had been carried off to Babylon in an earlier exile in 606 BC.

The prophecy written by Ezekiel can be best viewed as having three sections, each introduced with a date line: (1) Ezekiel 1–24, Before the siege of Jerusalem in 586 BC, (2) Ezekiel 25–32, During the days of the siege of Jerusalem, and (3) Ezekiel 33–48, After the siege of Jerusalem. Our Lord called Ezekiel "son of man" in this book one hundred times. He also appointed Ezekiel as a "Watchman" in Ezekiel 3:16-19 and again in 33:7. But most important of all is the fact that "The word of the LORD came to [Ezekiel]" forty-nine times in this book. This prophet delivered the messages from God as he stressed the holiness, power, and glory of God in his writing and preaching.

Moreover, Ezekiel demonstrated that he had received clear visions of what God was going to do in the future to the nation of Israel as it related to the conclusion of the world's leaders as they attempted to be sovereign over all nations and empires. Nowhere are these lines of demarcation between the rulers of this world and God's sovereignty over everything drawn more clearly than in the passage we have selected for this study: Ezekiel 21:18-27. This text calls us to focus on the world's future and its only legitimate and rightful ruler over all peoples and nations, viz., Yeshua, who is called the king of kings and LORD of lords.

THE BACKGROUND PASSAGE TO EZEKIEL 21:18-27 IN GENESIS 49:8-12

The patriarch Jacob had given the promise from God about his fourth son named Judah. There in the first book of the Torah Jacob compared his son Judah to a young lion, "You are a lion's cub, Judah, you return from the prey, my son, like a lion [that] crouches and lies down ... who dares to rouse him" (Gen 49:9). But there was more to this promise, for Jacob went on to say even more dramatically:

"The scepter will not depart from Judah, nor the ruler's staff from between his feet, until he to whom it belongs shall come and the obedience of the nations shall be his" (49:10).

The "scepter" was the symbol of the kingdom, throne and dynasty that ultimately would be given to that man God would choose who would come from the tribe of "Judah" named David, the son of Kish, in the future day of the Lord. Moreover, Jacob's sons will bow down to [this appointed one by God] (49:8c). Yes, and the one accurately called in Genesis 49:9b "my son" was called by the same name in Psalm 2:7 and in 2 Samuel 7:14; Psalm 89:26, 27; and Hebrews 1:5; he would be God's "son." However, there was a most difficult phrase in Genesis 49:8-12, and that was the reference to a certain "Shiloh" in verse 10c. But this phrase would become clear later when Ezekiel 21:27 rendered this cryptic word "Shiloh" as an abbreviated form for the clause rendered as: "until he to whom it rightfully belongs shall come." But how did the Biblical writer get from the word "Shiloh" to the clause: "until he to whom it rightfully belongs shall come?"

The phrase "until Shiloh comes" is best explained, we learn, if the Hebrew vowel pointing is changed from reading Shiloh to *shelloh* or *sheloh*, a change which is supported by thirty-eight Hebrew manuscripts.[57] Since the Hebrew vowel pointings are not part of the original text but were added to help those who had never heard the consonantal text read. When this change is examined, the word "*sheloh*" can be understood to be a Hebrew compound word "she," which is the shortened form of the relative particle "'*asher*," meaning "which," "whose," and Hebrew "*le*" means "belonging to" with the suffix "*-oh*" meaning "him." This accords exactly with the longer form or the clause that is spelled out in Ezekiel 21:27 [Hebrew, 32]. This rendering is also close to the way the Septuagint and Theodotion texts rendered "Shiloh" in Genesis 49:10, which texts read: "until that [meaning "dominion over the world"] comes which belongs to him [Judah]." With that in mind, let us look at the text in Ezekiel 21:18-27.

THE CONTEXT OF EZEKIEL 21:18-27 (HEBREW 21:23-32)

The section under review in Ezekiel 21:18-27 is preceded by two parables in Ezekiel 20:45-49 and 21:1-5. The first parable describes a forest fire in the southern part of the land of Israel—a fire that

57 See my fuller discussion in Kaiser, *The Messiah in the Old Testament*, 51-52.

consumes every tree, whether it is green or dry (20:47). The word for the "south" included Jerusalem and its sanctuary. But those who heard the prophet announce this parable of the sword dismissed him rather mockingly as they declared him to be a mere "spinner of parables" who insists on preaching metaphorically or in figurative speech.

Ezekiel then told another parable in 21:1-5 as he "set his face against Jerusalem." Yahweh would unsheathe his sword and its cutting edge would affect all in the land from the north to the south (21:4-5). The prophet is told to groan out loud in front of the people, which led them to ask what in the world was wrong with him (21:6). He answered that he was groaning for one reason, It happened because of the news that was coming soon, which announced that:

"Every heart will melt with fear and every hand go limp; every spirit will become faint, and every leg will be wet with urine. It is coming! It will surely take place, declares the Sovereign LORD" (21:7).

In verse 8 the prophet is told to sing a song about the sword—a sword that is sharpened, polished, and ready for slaughter. In fact, this sword will act with the speed of a lightning bolt (9-10a). The prophet is ordered to follow his verbal proclamation of God's promise of judgment with a dramatic and intense period of mourning and wailing with loud cries and with his beating on his chest or his thighs (21:12). The sword of the Lord is the instrument by which he will execute his sentence. This sword will surely create a panic among the people (21:15-17). This then serves as an introduction to our key text in Ezekiel 21:18-27.

THREE APPOINTMENTS OF THREE RULERS – 21:18-27 (HEBREW 21:23-32)

There can be little doubt that the key word is seen in the action of "appointing," for it appears in 21:19, 20, 22 [bis]. In fact, everything in these days described here are in a topsy-turvy state of confusion, yet it all is under a divine appointment. The three appointments are as follows:

I. ***God's Pagan Instrument of Judgment – 21:18-23***
II. ***God's Punished Ruler Deep in Sin – 21:24-25***
III. ***God's Rightful Ruler Over the Whole Universe – 21:26-27***

I. God's Pagan Instrument of Judgment – 2:18-23

Once again, as in the past, the first prophecy opens with an address to the prophet Ezekiel, "And you, son of man, prophesy and say, 'This is what the Sovereign LORD says about the Ammonites and their insults" (21:18).

This is sometimes called the prophetic "sword song," for it is further fortified with a series of imperatives that called for immediate action through its series of imperatives: "mark out ... two roads for the sword of the king of Babylon to take," "make a signpost (Hebrew, *yad*, "hand) where the road branched off to the city," "mark out one road for the sword to come against Rabbah of the Ammonites and [mark out] another [road] against Judah and fortified Jerusalem" (21:19-20).

Nebuchadnezzar would take this marked out route from Babylon until he came to Damascus, which is the most likely spot where he had to made a decision about whether he was going to go to the left first by taking a southern journey through Golan Heights east of the Jordan River, to deal with the Ammonites in their capital city of Rabbah, meaning the "Great City" (modern name Amman), which was located 23 miles east of the Jordan River and an important stop for salesmen traveling on the King's Highway, or was he going to go the right and take the road to Judah with its "enclosed" or "fortified" city of Jerusalem first.

Thus, the person Yahweh has chosen for this task of bringing his judgment on these two nations was Nebuchadnezzar. The Babylonian monarch was on a mission to correct both Judah and Ammon, who had both conspired against him in 598 BC to rebel against Babylon. God told the prophet that Nebuchadnezzar would stop at this key fork in the road and try to decide which of the two nations he would take on first; would it be Ammon, or would it be Judah? He hesitated in his progress, for he was uncertain about which way he was to proceed, therefore, in his customary Near Eastern habit, he decided to resort to his usual practice of divination to determine the mind of the gods on this matter, for that is why he decided "to seek an omen" (Hebrew, *qasam qesem*). The king of Babylon resorted to three methods of divination (cf. Isa 47:8-15). First, he resorted to casting lots by shaking the arrows in his quiver, which is known as "belomancy," or "rhabdomancy." Apparently, this method consisted of shaking two inscribed arrows on which were written the names to the two alternative sites he was going to attack, and then he would draw one of the two inscribed arrows out of the quiver just as one would draw a lot. Then in a second attempt to confirm this lot, "he consulted his idols" (21:21). This method was called consulting the "teraphim," but even though it was widely used in the Ancient Near East, we do not know much about it. A third method involved consulting a liver, which is known as "hepatoscopy," which is better known to us today, since we are in possession of a fairly large number of clay models of livers discovered in the second millennium site of Babylon inscribed with meanings for scars or signs on various parts of the liver being inspected (21:21d). Nebuchadnezzar was exceedingly superstitious and felt he needed the help of his gods to direct his course of action. However, the believer was warned early on to avoid all three (and more) of these practices in Deuteronomy 18:9-14. Anyway, the lot turned out to be that he was to go to the right in all three tests; he was directed to choose the road that would take him to Judah and Jerusalem.

However, the people of Judah argued with the prophet that this was a false prophecy and omen, for they correctly noted that they were not to take the results of divination seriously. Often the people would take some parts of the word of God very seriously when it was thought to be to their benefit. But they had a second objection, which they raised in Ezekiel 21:23; they were bound by an extremely solemn oath (here called "a sworn allegiance") that they had made to God, and he had made to them. But these same Judeans had already broken their agreement with Nebuchadnezzar, and they had also broken their oath with Yahweh. So, they did not have a leg to stand on! Judah was placing her confidence groundlessly in oaths they had continually broken.

It is significant that the plan of God should be confirmed even by those who would use methods that were so contrary to Scripture. But the point was this: Nothing, not even the works of the evil one, can overcome God's sovereign promise-plan in history!

II. God's Punished Ruler Deep in Sin – 21:24-25

The sins of this earthly monarch, who will be the last king in Israel and whose name was Zedekiah, will be exposed for his sin in the same three words used for sin in Psalm 32 and Exodus 34:6-7. There is the word "iniquity (Hebrew, *'avon*), meaning the crooked path of sin, the word "transgression" (Hebrew, *pesha'*), meaning the act of going beyond what God has said, and the word "to sin" (Hebrew, *hata'*), meaning "to miss the mark set by God."

The measure of king Zedekiah's guilt had become filled to the top of the cup that God was watching until it overflowed (cf. Gen 15:16; Ezek 7:2-3), for then it would be the time for God's threatened judgment to come.

III. God's Rightful Ruler – 21:26-27

The immediate context deals not exclusively with God's threatened judgment, as the non-Messianic interpreter's assert, but with the immediate prospect of the Davidic dynasty of Zedekiah being overturned and eliminated as stated explicitly in Ezekiel 21:25. So, while we are still talking about the divine appointments of all royalty on earth, this text is concerned particularly with the "wicked prince of Israel" (21:25).

In response to a second argument brought by the non-Messianic interpreters, the pronoun "this" in verse 25 does not refer to God's "judgment," as they argue,[58] but "this" points to a series of feminine pronouns in verses 26-27 that all refer to the same idea about to be opened. Moreover, how can God make "judgment" a "ruin" in verse 27a? Also, the nouns "turban" and "crown" are feminine nouns; therefore, the clause "this will not happen" does not speak to a "judgment" that will not come until this individual comes. Instead, it shows how the "turban" and the "crown" will no longer exist in Israel until God's special person comes.[59]

A third argument the non-Messianic interpreters propose is one that points out that the term "judgment" (Hebrew, *mishpat*) cannot denote something that is "right," as their messianic interpreters contend, for they fail to note the article on the term "the judgment," which the non-Messianic group sees as referring to the act of judgment. However, *mishpat* is used in this Ezekiel context of 21:27 to refer to the fact that the "turban" and "crown" will not exist in Israel again until the One comes to whom God has given it.

Ezekiel 21:27 is consistent with the meaning of Genesis 49:10. Ezekiel makes it clear that there will be a person for whom the believer's expectation is to wait for, and that one is non-other than Messiah and not Nebuchadnezzar. This is the way the prophets read these verses, including for example, Jeremiah 23:5; Zechariah 3:1-10, and 6:12-15.

---

58 The non-Messianic interpreters argue that the coming one is not Messiah, but he is Nebuchadnezzar, even though they acknowledge there is a connection of this passage with Genesis 49:10 as presenting a Messianic sort of undertone to the Ezekiel reference. Among those who take this view are Leslie C. Allen, *Ezekiel 20–48*, Word Biblical Commentary, vol. 29 (Dallas, Word, 1998) and Daniel I. Block, *The Book of Ezekiel 1–24*, The New International Commentary on the Old Testament (Grand Rapids, Eerdmans, 1997), 689.

59 This argument is cogently presented by Abner Chou, "Ezekiel 21:25-27: The Hope of Israel," *The Moody Handbook of Messianic Prophecy* (Chicago: Moody Publishers, 2019), 1074-75.

SUMMARY

Ezekiel 21:25-27 opens with the phrase "And you," meaning that our Lord has now shifted from discussing the sins and wickedness of his people now to deal specifically with King Zedekiah, the final ruler over Judah. He is called a "prince" because God does not regard him any longer as Judah's "king" (cf. 2 Kgs 24:17). Zedekiah is so "profane" that he is no longer able to stand in God's presence (Ezek 11:6; 20:9; also 6:4-7; 7:21-24). Therefore, the "day has come for [his] punishment;" the end has come for all of Zedekiah's sinful ways and for him too.

God next tells what that punishment will involve: the LORD will remove the turban and the crown from Zedekiah, which will end his office as king. However, since the term "turban" (Hebrew, *mitsenephet*) is used exclusively in the Old Testament to refer to the turban only worn by the high priest (Exod 28:4, 37, 39; Lev 8:9; 16:4), therefore the removal of the turban refers to the collapse of the priesthood. As a result, "things will remain as they are." Accordingly, the symbols of leadership in Israel will cease from Zedekiah onwards and will not come back again "until" the moment when Messiah comes back to earth again. Then it is that God will give "the judgment to [Messiah]" which refers to the "turban" and the "crown" as Messiah comes to take up the government on his shoulders and reign and rule forever as Priest and King.

CHAPTER 11

THE MESSIANIC KING WHO WILL RULE THE WORLD FROM JERUSALEM

ZECHARIAH 9:1–10:1

INTRODUCTION TO THE FOURTH BLOCK OF TEXTS: ZECHARIAH 9–14

The fourth and final block of messages in the book of Zechariah covers the last six chapters of the book—chapters 9–14. These chapters are divided into two equal sections: chapters 9–11 and 12–14. Each main block is introduced with the formula: "The burden of the word of the LORD" (9:1; 12:1). In general, the first "burden" emphasizes the first coming or advent of our Lord, while the second "burden" has as its main theme the second coming of our Messiah to this earth. Moreover, the first burden describes the rejection of the coming Messianic "Shepherd" (11:4-17) while the second burden demonstrates how Messiah will finally be recognized by Israel as a massive renewal takes place among the people of Israel (12:10–

13:10). Yes, and the tone of this fourth block of texts takes a change from the earlier portions, yet the chapters are not unrelated from the content of the previous eight.

Text: Zechariah 9:1-10:1

Focal Point: 9:9 "Rejoice greatly, Daughter of Zion! Shout, Daughter of Jerusalem! See, your king comes to you, righteous and victorious, lowly and riding on a donkey."

Title: "The Messianic King Who Will Govern the World from Jerusalem"

Homiletical Keyword: GOALS

Interrogative: WHAT? (are the GOALS this Messianic King will exercise as he governs the kingdom of God?)

Outline:

I. He Will Be Preceded by the Onslaught of Alexander The Great's Victories – 9:1-8

II. He Will Come in His First Advent as a Humble King and Savior – 9:9

III. He Will Come in His Second Advent to Establish His World-Wide Kingdom – 9:10-17

The Lesson:

I. He Will Be Preceded by the Onslaught of Alexander The Great's Victories – 9:1-8

The first coming of our Lord will be set up in many ways by the mind-boggling conquests of the Greek Macedonian General named "Alexander the Great" in the fourth century BC. That is why the form this prophecy takes is accurately entitled a "burden," which noun comes from the Hebrew root *nasa`*, "to lift up." Therefore, this was a message that carried a threat and an admonition.[60] It was not an "oracle," as all too many want the English translations incorrectly to translate the term! Instead, it carried a heavy message of judgment, therefore it was not just an "Oracle."

This prophecy begins with a word against the land of "Hadrach," a name which only occurs here in Scripture. At one time this term was a real mystery, but it can now be identified as the Hatarika, which is mentioned in the Annals of the Assyrian kings as an Aramean country near Damascus and Hamath on the Orontes River, against which Assyria campaigned in 772, 755, and 733 BC.

Thus, the general region of Damascus is named as the area where the prophet envisions a coming battle in the hinterland of the Anti-Lebanon mountains near Damascus and Syria. In fact, that is what later happened at the battle of Issus, in southeastern Asia Minor, on October 333 BC. Alexander the Great inflicted a heavy defeat on Darius and the Persians, which then opened up all of Syria and all of Canaan to his blitzkrieg type of warfare. The prophet had indeed envisioned the defeat of Judah's traditional enemies: first Damascus, Hamath, and then the cities, such as Tyre and Sidon, which were inside the Syrian interior along the coast.

A detachment of Alexander's army conquered Hadrach, with its key towns, Damascus and Hamath, as the prophet pictured it happening, in "the eyes of all the people" (9:1), along with the eyes of "all the tribes of Israel," which were focused on the Lord. Apparently, what this meant was that when the eyes of all the Gentiles and Israel gazed on what Alexander was doing, they were actually focusing on the Lord who was behind all that was going on through the armies of Alexander.

Verses 2b-4 focused on Tyre and Sidon, for they were singled out for special mention because of their great wealth, prosperity, and worldly wisdom. The opulence and pride of Tyre were at times

60 E. W. Hengstenberg. *Christology of the Old Testament* (Grand Rapids: Kregel, 1956), 3:339-43. See Also Walter C. Kaiser, Jr., "Massa,' in *Theological Wordbook of the Old Testament*, eds. R. Laird Harris, Gleason L Archer, Jr., and Bruce K. Waltke (Chicago: Moody, 1980), 2:602.

overbearing; in fact, so overbearing that the prophet Ezekiel gave one grand extended treatment of such contempt for Tyre in Ezekiel in 28:2-8, 11-19. The name Tyre probably comes from the Hebrew *tsor*, meaning "rock," which she had built for herself as a "bulwark/ stronghold" (Hebrew *matsor*, perhaps a pun on the name for Tyre [?]).

Tyre had such wealth that its silver was said to be heaped up like dust and her gold was like "mire," or "mud," in the streets (9:3). It surely was plentiful.

The secular historian Diodorus Siculus mentioned that Babylonian ruler named Nebuchadnezzar had been unsuccessful in his thirteen years (572 BC) in attempting to lay siege and conquer Tyre, as had the Assyrian King Shalmaneser, who likewise had proven to be unsuccessful in his previous five-year siege of Tyre. But Tyre, in a haughty manner, just simply picked up all her stuff and moved one-half mile out into the Mediterranean Sea to an island fortification just off the coast of the city, where she made a new city for herself. Moreover, they surrounded insular Tyre with a wall 150 feet high, so she felt really secure. However, Alexander the Great was not to be denied a victory by this proud city of Tyre, for Alexander merely scraped up the ruins of the decimated and deserted mainland city, dumped all of this trash and its timbers, stones, rubbish and anything left of the old residence into the Mediterranean Sea, and built a causeway, or a mole, out into the sea over which he marched his army and his siege machines as he quickly took the unconquerable Tyre in 332 BC. It took Alexander only seven months to complete the action, which was an improvement on Shalmaneser's five years and Nebuchadnezzar's thirteen years of hard siege work, but both of those previous attempts had been with little results, for they were denied success.

Few prophecies in the Old Testament are fulfilled more dramatically in detail about her capture than this one about Tyre (cf., Ezek 26:12). In fact, this passage in Ezekiel literally says:

"They will break down your walls and demolish your fine houses and throw your stones, timber and rubble into the sea."

Alexander was clearly given divine wisdom and an impressive strategy from the Lord himself, for verse 4 introduced this concept with an interjectional adverb, "Look/Behold the LORD will take away her possessions and destroy her power on the sea, and she will be consumed by fire." Hence the LORD "drove out" the Tyrians and he took possession of their commercial island-center. The mole that Alexander created out to the island city of Tyre was never removed, but it tended to be covered over with more sand deposits over the succeeding years so that it remains visible to this very day, forming what was an island into as sort of peninsula with something like a half-mile wide land bridge to the mainland today.

Alexander moved from conquering the northern sites of Phoenicia to take on the southern cities of Philistia. Four of the five Philistine Pentapolis are named here as captured: Ashkelon, Ashdod, Ekron, and Gaza; however, the city of Gath is usually removed later in its history from this famous list of five cities because it belonged, at least for a period of time, to Judah. No special details of Alexander's march against Ashdod, Ekron, or Ashdod are given in Scripture, but the outcome of the battle for Gaza is fully and unmercifully recorded. Gaza's king, Batis, was ruthlessly slain as he was dragged through the streets attached to a chariot with thongs thrust through the soles of his feet. Moreover, ten thousand of Gaza's inhabitants were slaughtered as well by Alexander's army according to historical records.

Batis was called a king, for apparently the Persians had allowed Gaza's own local ruler to be a sort of sub-king under the Persian monarch, who himself was styled the "king of kings." However, God would cut off the "pride of the Philistines" (6b) and "a mongrel people will occupy Ashdod" predicted the LORD (6a). God would also take away the "blood" of the idolatrous sacrifices of the Philistines (7). Thus, judgment fell on the neighboring enemies of Israel, but God would "encamp" around his people to protect them and preserve them for the coming of the Messiah.

There is a rather remarkable fulfillment of the first part of verse

8 recorded in Josephus' *Antiquities of the Jews* (XI.8:3). It happened that Alexander had demanded of the Jewish High Priest Jaddua the payment that Judah had customarily given in the past as tribute to the king of Persia. But Jaddua refused to break his oath of loyalty to the Persian King Darius, which caused Alexander to threaten severe punishments on Jerusalem. He would carry out his threats on Jerusalem after he was finished dealing with Tyre and the Philistine cities.

Jaddua, however, ordered the people of Jerusalem to make sacrifices to God and to pray for deliverance from Alexander's onslaughts. God gave the high priest Jaddua a dream in which he was instructed to go out of the city of Jerusalem to welcome Alexander, which is what he did in his full robe and insignias. Thus, the Macedonian conqueror was met by the Jewish High Priest clothed in purple and scarlet, with a miter on his head made with its golden plate and the name of God inscribed on it. He was followed by priests clothed in their white robes.

Amazingly enough, Alexander also spoke of having had a dream just prior to this event, in which he had seen just such a person when he was at Dios in Macedonia. Consequently, Alexander treated the Jews kindly, and the city of Jerusalem was granted the self-same deliverance Zechariah had relayed in his prophecy in verse 8. For God himself had announced that he himself would "encamp about his house because of an army." His "house" stood, by the figure of speech known as a metonymy, a figure of speech for the whole land of Israel, or his people living in that land. The "army," of course, was the army of Alexander the Great. Thus Judah was supernaturally spared by two dreams given to two different leaders—one to Jaddua and the other to Alexander!

II. He Will Come in His First Advent as a Humble King and Savior – 9:9

Verses 1-8 traced the victorious progress of the Gentile world conqueror Alexander the Great, which God would use as his own rod of chastisement on Israel's enemies while he delivered the people and land of Israel by encamping round about them. Thus, at the heart of chapter 9 stands one of the most famous predictions about the coming of the Messianic king. As such, then, it functions as the pivotal point between verses 1-8 and 11-17.

The prophet begins by urging the people of Jerusalem, here personified as "the daughter of Zion" and "the daughter of Jerusalem" "to rejoice greatly" and to "shout" (9). The reason for all this commotion is that earth will finally receive the first advent of her coming king. So, it is time for "Joy to the World, the Lord has come," as Psalm 98 will put it as well and Isaac Watts agreed in the words of his famous Christmas Carol of "Joy to the World." Previously, the prophet Zechariah has issued the same call for jubilation in Zechariah 3:14-15: "Sing, O daughter of Zion! Shout, O Israel.... The King of Israel is in your midst." That same word, which was in Zechariah 2:10 as well appears here in verse 9. Messiah's arrival would be cause for heaps of joy!

But with the word about his arrival came a description of the character of this coming kingly Messiah at another time (9d-f). First, he would be "righteous," i.e., one who would be animated by maintaining and displaying his righteous rule with justice and fairness all the time. Secondly, he would come "having salvation." Here the verb is used in its passive form, meaning the Messiah has experienced the Father's deliverance and victory. Thirdly, Messiah is described as being "lowly," one showing "humility" and identity with the poor and the disenfranchised. To illustrate this, Messiah would come "riding on a donkey, on a colt, the foal of a donkey." Contrary to how the donkey is regarded in the west, in the ancient Near East the donkey was not thought of as a lowly beast of burden, but as a preferred mount of choice for princes (Judg 5:10; 10:4; 12;14), or the mount of kings (2 Sam 16:1-2). Horses, especially when hitched to chariots, were viewed as instruments of war (Deut 17:16; Ps 33:16-17; Isa 33:1). Therefore, the fact that Messiah did not come in his first advent on a horse signified that he would not come, at least at this time, as a conqueror. Instead, Messiah would come as promised in Genesis 49:11, mounted on a donkey—his coming would signal peace in the latter days to come and for all eternity.

Two of the Synoptic Gospels, Matthew 21:2-7 and John 12:12-15, connect this prophecy with the triumphal entry of Yeshua into Jerusalem on Palm Sunday. John notes that Jesus rode on the "young" animal, while Matthew notes that both the donkey and the colt were brought for Jesus' use. As he would later enter Jerusalem, the crowds would shout "Hosanah," "Save now!" They would cut down branches and spread their coats out as a carpet for Jesus to ride on. This prophecy would be literally fulfilled—and that is what happened!

III. He Will Come in His Second Advent to Establish His World-Wide Kingdom – 9:10-17

After treating the first advent of Jesus' arrival in Jerusalem, we turn now to our Lord's second advent in verses 10-17. Immediately, our Lord calls for the abolishment of three weapons of war: "the chariots from Ephraim," "the war-horses from Jerusalem," and "the battle bow" (10). God's kingdom would not be founded on worldly might or military power, for the Prince of Peace certainly would not be delivered from those who were hostile to him by means of chariots and horses and their armies. The mention of "Ephraim" and "Jerusalem" was but one more reminder that the northern and southern kingdoms of the Israelite kingdom that had been split apart in twain since 931 BC would in that coming day be reunified and restored back as one nation once again.

The Prince of Peace would not only benefit Israel and Judah, but "he shall proclaim peace to the nations" (10d) as well. The result would be that "His rule will extend from sea to sea and from the River (i.e., the Euphrates) to the ends of the earth" (10e-f). This is a quotation from Psalm 72, a psalm which again Isaac Watts celebrated in his hymn, "Jesus Shall Reign Wher'er the Sun Does Its Successive Journeys Run." His kingdom would, in other words, extend over the whole globe! It would be worldwide!

The last seven verses of the chapter 9 discuss the results and mission of the Redeemer-King, especially as they pertain to Israel nationally. The section begins with "As for you" (11a), which links verses 11-13 with 9-10. And everything that will happen in that future day—the arrival of Messiah and his rule and reign as absolute Lord over all—will have been made possible by "the blood of my covenant" (11a), a phrase that occurs only one other time in Scripture (Exod 24:8), although the Old Testament referred often to the idea of a blood sacrifice when the covenant was ratified with Abraham (e.g.. Gen 15:9-11) or with Moses (Exod 24:8). These words, however, seem very familiar to us, for Jesus used them at the institution of the Last Supper in Mark 14:24: "This is my blood of the new covenant, which is shed for many." What, then, did the "blood" refer to?

Blood in these contexts does not refer as it does in our modern times to a transfusion that would impart sustained life to the one to whom it was donated; instead, it signifies that the life was in the blood (Lev 17:11) and that which was spilt on the ground in death as a substitute life for those who whose debt was paid for by the one presenting the sacrificial offering.

Because of the substituted life that has been yielded up on our behalf, God promises that he "will free your prisoners from the waterless pit" (11b). This reference to the "waterless pit" apparently was odd to some, for it was omitted in the NEB and bracketed in the JB versions. However, the point was this: since there were no jails in that day, cisterns that were normally used to collect rain water during the rainy season also often had to double at times as a retention center, or a jail for the convicted felons. Thus, Joseph was cast into a "pit" that had no water in it (Gen 37:24), as was the prophet Jeremiah (Jer 38:6-13). But our Lord promises to empty these pits or jails in that coming day. Those so released, Zechariah dubs as "prisoners of hope" (12a). They will surely return to the "fortress," i.e., back to Zion once again. In so doing, God will "restore twice as much to [them]" (12b), just as the "firstborn" would receive a double inheritance (Deut 21:17).

God would involve Judah and Ephraim in his liberation of the captives. He would rouse Zion's sons against the sons of Greece/Javan (13c), a prediction perhaps of the Maccabean wars in a later period of Israel's history. But the Lord will protect his people under the figure of a storm (14).

The chapter closes with a description of a banquet of the released prisoners. The language appears somewhat odd and has led some to incorrectly think that the prisoners were eating flesh or drinking the blood of their enemies. However, the eating and drinking in this context are used as metaphors for celebrating Yahweh's victory over the nations. Likewise, the "slingstones" (15) are mere reminders of previous battles, but whose stones are now no more than gravel to be trampled underfoot.

So abundant will the food be at the victory celebration that "they will drink and roar as with wine" (15c). In fact, the tables will be so full of food that they will look like an altar appears when the meat on it overflows even into the corners of the altar.

Verse 16a continued by saying, "On that day" Yahweh will save his people and as a result his "flock" will be safe. They will "sparkle in his land like jewels in a crown." Here was another metaphor that came from Exodus 19:5, where the believing remnant would be God's "treasured possession," which signified movable treasures as opposed to real estate that could not be moved (cf. Mal 3:17). Together, grain and wine would be abundant in that day. Evil will have been vanquished forever and the Lord God would be in charge (Amos 9:13; Joel 3:18).

Yes, the prosperity of those days would depend on rain, so 10:1 urged that the people of God should "ask the LORD for rain in the time of the latter rain" (10:1). The promise was if the people asked, the Lord would send showers of rain and there would be plants of the field for everyone. This would be a different day indeed!

SUMMARY

The Messiah king will initiate drastic changes as He exhibits true righteousness. He will exemplify a paid-for salvation and a humility of purpose as he rides into Jerusalem on a donkey as the promised Man of Promise! Messiah's second return as the king of kings and Lord of lords will bring even more cataclysmic changes making Alexander's victories pale in comparison to the victories of King Jesus over all nations. The Messianic Prince of Peace will come for all Israel and for all the nations as promised.

CHAPTER 12

ELIJAH, JOHN THE BAPTIST, THE TWO WITNESSES, AND THE FIRST AND SECOND COMING OF MESSIAH

REVELATION 11:3-19

Elijah not only served his own day and his own times in a powerful way, but under the appointment of God he was also designated by the same Lord to be a harbinger and an earnest of one who would function as a sort of a down-payment on what was yet to be realized in the history of this world in connection with that coming great and dreadful day of the Lord. Elijah, it turns out, more than any other person in the history of the ongoing story of God's plan for the world, demonstrated what could be expected from himself in the end days as well as what could be expected from those leaders who were filled with the Holy Spirit and the power of God, as well as could be expected of Messiah himself!

Accordingly, God would use Elijah in that future day of the Lord as he had in the past. After all, had not the last prophet of the Old Testament, the prophet Malachi, predicted: "Behold, I will send you Elijah the prophet before the great and dreadful day of the Lord comes?" (Mal 4:5).

ELIJAH AS A PROTOTYPE OF THE COMING OF JOHN THE BAPTIST

Elijah's work apparently was not finished when our Lord took him up to heaven in a whirlwind. We catch a glimpse of this when the disciples of Jesus asked our Lord very directly if the prophet Elijah was going to come back to earth and precede his second arrival as the Messiah of Israel: "Why do the scribes say that first Elijah must come?" Our Lord's answer at first sounded as if it were a bit of "double-talk," for he replied: "Elijah is coming [present tense] and he is to restore all things; but I tell you that Elijah has already come and they did to him whatever they pleased .... Then the disciples understood that he was speaking about John the Baptist" (Matt 17:11-13; Mark 9:13). The disciples had therefore gained an understanding of what the prophecy meant that predicted Elijah must precede the coming of our Lord, but it seems they, in their understanding, only got a piece of it correct.

But we still need more data before we can understand today more fully what our Lord was pointing to when he mentioned a coming of Elijah and how John the Baptist fitted into this picture. So, when John the Baptist was asked straight out if he were Elijah, his answer was just as straightforward: "No." John was quizzed further, "Are you a prophet?" Again, he simply answered, "No." They were really puzzled now all the more, for they asked John in frustration, "Who are you then?" John's answer was this: "I am a voice crying in the wilderness; 'Prepare the way of the Lord.'" (John 1:21). John, of course, was appealing to the prophetic words of Isaiah 40:3 ("The voice of one calling: in the desert prepare the way for the LORD."). The Baptizer was to be a herald of the coming Messiah; he would be the one who would prepare the way for Messiah's coming!

There is no contradiction In Jesus,' or Scripture's words, or that the text of Scripture, or even that the Holy Spirit, who gave the Scriptures on whether John the Baptizer was indeed that predicted coming messenger formerly named Elijah or not. For Jesus added on another occasion: "For all the Law and the Prophets prophesied until John [the Baptist]; and if you are willing to accept it, he is Elijah who is to come" (Matt 11:13, 14). That clears up part of this puzzle, for Jesus regarded John the Baptizer as the fulfillment of that prophecy, both in the sense of one who already fulfilled the prediction about Elijah who was to come, and yet in a more extended sense, John's coming did not completely fulfill the entire prophecy, for it fell short of the total historical fulfillment of this divine word in this Scripture.

This is why it is all the more important that we see in what sense John fulfilled the prophecy, for in order to do that we must also include the pledge the angel made at the announcement of the birth of John the Baptist. John, the angel affirmed, would go forth before the Lord "in the spirit and the power of Elijah" (Luke 1:17). There is the key which helps us to see how John the Baptist could have fulfilled the prediction about Elijah's coming, and yet we can also see how John could not have fulfilled everything the prophet Malachi had in mind when he gave his prediction about Elijah's future coming in that last day.

To understand this, we must realize that prophecy in the Bible often has both a "now" aspect and a "not yet" side to its predictions (1 John 3:2). Willis J. Beecher taught much the same when he announced and described what he called "Generic Predictions," which he carefully defined in this manner:

> A generic prediction is one which regards an event as occurring in a series of parts, separated by intervals, and expresses itself in language that may apply indifferently to

> the nearest part, or to the remoter parts, or to the whole—in other words, a prediction which, in applying to the whole of a complex event, also applies to some of its parts.[61]

The idea here is that some prophecies point to a final, climactic event, but often that event is itself part of a previous series of events, all of which participate in or lead up to the climactic event. What embraces this series of parts is not some sort of double sense, i.e., an alleged double meaning of the text of Scripture, or some spiritual, mystical, or deeper meaning, which escaped the purview of the writer of Scripture, but the fact that at times Scripture set its teachings in persons or things in concepts that had what is known as a "corporate or collective solidarity." Accordingly, to give an example, the prophecy about the coming "Seed" that was part of God's promise-plan for this world, which includes in the one word "seed" not only the promise of a coming One, who is the Messiah (Gal 3:16), but it often entailed as well as all who will accept Messiah by faith and constitute the one people of the promise plan of God! Thus, Scripture would seem to oscillate between the "One" and the "many" in its use of such terms as the "seed," yet these writers saw a solidarity and a unity of oneness in such a collective or corporate term!

Joel's promise of the "Day of the Lord" is another good example of such a generic prediction of the One and the Many. Peter stood up in front of the crowd and spoke about the "day of the Lord" on the day of Pentecost and affirmed: "This is [that which, or] what was spoken by the prophet Joel" (Acts 2:16-21; Joel 2:16). That seemed to have settled the matter as far as Joel's audience was concerned—for as it was being fulfilled at Pentecost, it became the day Joel had meant when he spoke as far back as perhaps the ninth century BC of the "day of the Lord." However, note that its fulfillment came as much as eight centuries after Joel made this prediction, for Peter also spoke these same words on the day of Pentecost. However, Peter

---

61 Willis J. Beecher, *The Prophets and the Promise* (New York: Crowell, 1905; Grand Rapids, Baker, 1963), 130.

applied only the first two verses of that prediction, but he did not include the next two verses that spoke about "wonders in the heavens and on earth, blood and fire and billows of smoke." Nor was the "sun turned into darkness" or "the moon [in]to blood." Even though those words were part of the prophecy, they were not fulfilled on the day of Pentecost—there was more to come, which the Pentecost of Peter's day did not complete!

This same point can be made about other prophecies, such as the ones about the coming of the terrible Antichrist. Already John had warned that "many antichrists had come" thus far in history (1 John 2:18), even though Antiochus Epiphanes IV had appeared in 167 BC and exhibited part of the fulfillment of this prophecy, as many modern dictators such as Hitler and his type exhibited. Thus, just as a Messianic line of David's descendants came in that line of descendants who came one after the other until Messiah would come, so there would be a line of power-grabbers and God-haters throughout history, each who could be truthfully called the "antichrist" until that final one in that predicted line arrived in a future day of the Lord.[62] In this way Elijah would indeed come in a more godly line before the great and dreadful day of the Lord yet in the future!

ELIJAH THE PROPHET APPEARED DURING MINISTRY OF JESUS

It happened just one week after the famous incident that took place at Caesarea-Philippi, near the base of Mount Hermon, where the disciple Peter had made his awesome confession of our Lord in answer to Jesus' question to his disciples, "Who do you say I am?" Peter famously volunteered, "You are Messiah, the Son of the living God" (Matt 16:16). Jesus praised Peter for his correct answer, but

62 Walter C. Kaiser, Jr, "The Prophetic Use of the Old Testament in the New," in *The Uses of the Old Testament in the New* (Chicago: Moody, 1985), 61-100.

then cautioned him to remember that he was able to say this, not because of his own ingenuity, or his superior knowledge, but as a revelation that had come from his Father in heaven.

One week later, Jesus took Peter, James, and John up into the mountain of his transfiguration by themselves, as our Lord began to fortify himself for the great spiritual and physical ordeal that was to take place involving him in Jerusalem, where he would be hauled off to be brutally crucified. Once on that mountain of Transfiguration, Jesus began to prepare for this crisis by entering into the work of prayer. As he was praying, suddenly he was transfigured right before their eyes (Matt 17:1-8; Mark 9:2-8; Luke 9:28-36). So radiant was the change that took place in Jesus as he was praying that he was transfigured in front of the three disciples and "his face shone as the sun" (Matt 17:2). In that moment, the Shekinah glory broke out on the face of the One who himself was and is the Glory of God. Thus, this outburst of brilliance was but a brief anticipation of that glory that was soon to be shown to be his on a permanent basis—the glory he had with the Father, but which glory he had laid aside voluntarily when he left heaven to come to earth, that is until he had finished the work God the Father had sent him to accomplish here on earth.

Jesus' clothes became dazzling white and bright as a flash of lightning. Such a brilliance must have been resplendent against the backdrop of the dark blue sky. In so doing, our Lord provided another reminder of those numerous appearances of the Son of Man throughout the Old Testament, such as the pillar of fire by night which became the cloud of glory by day, the burning bush that did not consume the bush, the thunders and lightnings on Mount Sinai, along with those times when the Lord entered Israel's battles and magnificently fought for her.

Suddenly, two men appeared with Jesus: Moses and the prophet Elijah! If we should ask, "Why were these two men chosen to be here?" The answer undoubtedly was to affirm the glory, dignity, and assured success of our Lord before he faced the darkest hour he or this world had seen up to that point. The enormous shame, ignominy, and disgrace needed to be counterbalanced and set over against the blazing glory that was anticipated in the triumphal conclusion of Yeshua in his death and resurrection in Jerusalem.

Moreover, to answer the question more directly, Moses appeared with our Lord as one who represented the one who was the founder of the law; he who had the power to accomplish such through the Father, as well as to turn the water into blood and to smite the earth with every plague. Elijah, on the other hand, represented the one who under God the Father was given the power to shut up the heavens so that it did not rain. In many ways he was at the head of the whole line of heaven-sent prophets These two key mortals from Israel's past entered into conversation with Yeshua, the Messiah, on that mountain in the presence of the three disciples.

But what could their conversation have been about? Luke tells us that the topic of their conversation was nothing less than the "exodus" or "departure" that Jesus was to accomplish shortly in Jerusalem (Luke 9:31). Great leaders talk with a great God on great topics! Such a topic of conversation, then, should be no surprise, for the salvation of the two representatives as well as the three disciples was dependent on what was going to happen as a result of this "departure," just as much as our own salvation was part of the event that was to take place shortly in Jerusalem. Their only hope lay exactly where ours lies—in the work of Messiah on their behalf. Had Yeshua not died for all our sin, all the saving grace that had been promised and shown to so many converts in the pre-cross moments in a proleptic and promissory way would have been ineffective and valueless!

Moses and Elijah were not singled out because they were some sort of super saints, or that they were mortals who were sinless. In fact, it was already recorded in Scripture how petulant Moses had been on several occasions, and how fretful and cowardly Elijah had acted after the Mount Carmel event. But when they get together, as we noted already, great men talk about great themes and so they together discussed the theme of redemption which Messiah would accomplish in a matter of days.

Moses may well have dwelt on how Yeshua must die as the lamb of God, the goat whose blood was shed on the Day of Atonement. True, the blood of bulls and goats could never take away sin (Heb 10:1-2), but neither did the first testament claim that that was possible, nor did it teach that the blood mentioned in Leviticus did take away sins. Instead, it argued that that forgiveness was available as the gift from God; the sin offerings that accompanied divine forgiveness were merely pictures and representative of that special work which was yet to come in the shed blood of Yeshua on the cross.

No less exciting must have been the contribution from the prophet Elijah. He too most assuredly must have contributed to this elevated conversation with the Living God by talking about the glory that should now belong to God the Father, the glory that would come when Yeshua had accomplished all that God the Father had planned from eternity past. The same glory that had thundered down on Mount Carmel in the contest where either Baal or Yahweh was to demonstrate that one or the other was the real God, that was the glory which Elijah witnessed on Mount Carmel when the fire of God dramatically fell on Elijah's sacrifice. This was the same glory Elijah had caught a glimpse of at the mouth of the cave on Mount Sinai as he was summoned in his deeply despondent mood to watch the majesty of the glory of the God with all its might and power "pass by" in front of him! God's prophet Elijah needed a new view of the majesty of an awesome God! This was the same glory that would now break out on Easter Sunday morning and radiate all over the earth with unsurpassed brilliance and majesty when the crowds shouted: "He is risen, He is risen indeed!"

All of this and more Moses and Elijah had talked about with the Lord, all of which was well known to our Lord, for, after all, it was he who had first given it to them under the inspiration of the Holy Spirit. Nevertheless, these were the identical topics that must also have strengthened and gladdened the heart of our Lord as he now faced the darkest moment that heaven ever has seen or ever will face.

What Moses and Elijah experienced on the Mount of Transfiguration was a review of what they had known in their walk with God, as well as an earnest or a harbinger of what was to come in the future work of Messiah. Of all the possible topics that that conversation on the mount could have selected, all would have been dwarfed by the magnitude of Yeshua's death and his resurrection centered in this conversation about his "departure" or "exodus" that was soon to occur.

In the New Testament, there are some 175 passages that focus on the death of Yeshua. The point must be made, therefore, that the closer we get to the cross in our theology and its emphases, the closer we come to the heart and center of our faith in Messiah and his triumphal conclusion to all he has planned for those who love him.

THE APPEARANCE OF THE TWO WITNESSES IN REVELATION 11:3-19

There is one more episode in our study of the life of Elijah we must examine in order to complete our study of Elijah and the Messiah; it is in Revelation 11:3-19. Of course, some believers tend to get nervous when the subject of study becomes the book of Revelation, but such nervousness is unnecessary, for the final book in the New Testament is primarily a book of worship; it is "the revelation of Jesus Christ" (Rev 1:1). The scene that dominates the whole book of Revelation is the throne of God (Rev 4–5).

But what is of special interest to us in the study of Elijah is Revelation 11, which records the narrative about the two witnesses. It is true, of course, that this episode does not say that one of the witnesses is Elijah the prophet, but it does say that "these men have power to shut the sky so that it will not rain during the time they are prophesying, and they have power to turn waters into blood and to strike the earth with every kind of plague as often as they want" (Rev 11:6). This description strongly suggests that Moses and Elijah are empowered by God to come back to earth again in that last day and to use the powers they had been empowered to use while on earth previously.

The message of Revelation 11 is that these two men will stand up in Jerusalem and preach repentance for 1,260 days (approximately three and a half years of 30-day-months in the Jewish lunar calendar). These two witnesses are the same two who are pictured in the book of Zechariah who stood before the Lord to serve God, so the two witnesses will stand before God to witness for him just before the great climax in history arrives in the Second Advent of Messiah.

The interesting point is that the emphasis of Zechariah 4:3 is precisely where it was in the lives of Elijah and the John the Baptist. Zechariah announced in that amazing text: "[It is] not by might, nor by power, but by my Spirit, says the LORD of Hosts." And that is where the matter still rests in our day as well. It is still a matter of the infilling of the Holy Spirit and the indwelling power from God that we today can carry out the mission of the Yeshua (cf. Luke 1:17). Did not Elijah's successor, the prophet Elisha, pray for a double portion of Elijah's spirit (2 Kgs 2:9)?

The story does not end there, however. These two witnesses in that final day were not unopposed, for suddenly the "beast" in Revelation 11:7 appears. He is easily identified as the person known as "the man of lawlessness" (2 Thess 2:3), or as the "little horn" in Daniel 7:21. This monster will come up from the abyss to attack, oppose, overpower, and kill the two witnesses who will be preaching the gospel. Not only will he kill them, but he will leave their bodies in the streets of Jerusalem to rot for three and a half days (Rev 11:8). So relieved will the contemporary men and women representing every people, tribe, language and nation be at the event of their death that they will stare and gawk at their dead bodies, and they will send gifts to one another, as if it were Christmas (Rev 11:9, 10).

After the bodies had lain rotting in the streets for three and a half days, suddenly, in the midst of all the partying and giving of gifts to each other on their success of finally silencing these two evangelists of repentance, God will grant his two witnesses life and vitality once again. We can only imagine the absolute shock and unmitigated consternation that this sudden change will bring world-wide—the mockers will be stunned and thunder-struck as never before.

This will be followed by a loud voice that will direct them to "Come up here!" (Rev 11:12), as they disappear from mortal's sight and ascend to heaven in a cloud, as their enemies gawk at them with wide open mouths at such a spectacular event taking place right before their eyes.

In that very same hour there will be an earthquake that appears to be of epic proportions (11:13), wherein a tenth part of the city of Jerusalem will just plain "collapse" and 7,000 people will be killed, leaving the survivors "terrified" and "giv[ing] glory to the God of heaven" (11:13b). With this event loud voices will shout from heaven:

"The kingdom of this world has become the kingdom of our Lord and of his Christ, and he will reign for ever and ever" (11:15b).

Earth's finest hour had indeed come! Then it will be that our Lord will grasp his power and his rightful authority, as he begins his reign over all nations and all the universe and all creatures (11:17). With that, the temple in heaven will be opened and there will be seen the Ark of his Covenant (11:19)! After so many had cried out so often, "How long O Lord," this will be one very satisfying and extremely spectacular works of God. This finale to earth's history will be greater than any super-bowl football game or even any conceivable awesome event on planet earth.

Is it any wonder, then, that we find all that is so central and dear to us as believers in the work God did in the life of Elijah? Elijah truly was and still is the forerunner of our Lord Messiah and his awesome glory. As James told us, Elijah is more than rightfully held forth as a model of effective prayer in James 5:12, for look what such prayer was party to! He also functions easily as one of the *sina qua non* examples of a faithful witness to the gospel and the person of our Lord Jesus Christ.

SUMMARY

Prayer obviously was the secret of Elijah's power, as James 5:12 argues. This surely must be a guideline for us in our day as well. John the Baptizer shared about the Spirit and power that Elijah possessed (Luke 1:17) as could be seen in John's short ministry of six months in which he performed not even one miracle, yet he spoke mightily the word of God. The interaction that took place on the Mount of Transfiguration was both encouraging and strengthening not only to Yeshua, but to Moses and Elijah as well. Moses had a special contribution and Elijah had another, but both will also be a part of the soon-to-happen event of participating in our complete redemption. In addition, the two witnesses of the Revelation 11:3-19 again feature Moses and Elijah. God began his gift of revelation by giving his word and he will conclude it in that final day the same way.

CONCLUSION

The Jesus I know: Yeshua the Messiah develops God's plan for the predicted Messiah of the Old Testament as the longed-for King of the World. The book overviews *Yeshua* starting with Genesis 3:15 up through the book Revelations as *Yeshua* is portrayed as the center of God's story and the center for biblical theology. *Yeshua* is seen as the Branch and culmination of the Davidic royal grant promise of 2 Samuel 7 and He is also presented in the Scripture as the One Who will suffer humiliation and yet be triumphal as the messianic Psalms and prophets predict. Messiah will return as foretold in the OT and will rule the world from Jerusalem. We eagerly await his glorious return to eradicate all vestiges of the sin and the curse.

BIBLIOGRAPHY

Allis, O. T. "The Blessing of Abraham," *Princeton Theological Review* 25, 1927: 263-98.

Allis, O. T. *Prophecy and the Church*. Philadelphia: Presbyterian and Reformed, 1945.

Anderson, A. A. *The Book of Psalms*. 2 vols. New Century Bible Commentary. Grand Rapids: Eerdmans, 1972.

Baron, David. *Rays of Messiah's Glory: Christ in the Old Testament*. Grand Rapids: Zondervan reprint of 1886: n.d.

Becker, Joachim. *Messianic Expectations in the Old Testament*, trans. David E. Green (Philadelphia: Fortress, 1980.

Beecher, Willis J. *The Prophets and the Promise*. New York: Crowell, 1905; reprint Grand Rapids, Baker, 1963, 1970.

Briggs, Charles A. *Messianic Prophecy*. New York: Charles Scribner's Sons, 1889.

Brueggemann, Walter and Miller, Patrick D. "Psalm 73 as Canonical Marker," *JSOT* 72, 1996: 45-56.

Culver, Robert D. *The Sufferings and the Glory of the Lord's Righteous Servant*. Moline, IL: Christian Service Foundation, 1958.

Dahood, Mitchell. *Psalms, vol. 2:51-100*. Anchor Bible. Garden City, NY: Doubleday, 1968.

Delitzsch, Franz. *Isaiah: Commentary on the Old Testament* 2 vols. Grand Rapids: Eerdmans, reprint 1973.

Dhorme, E. A. *Commentary on the Book of Job*, trans. Harold Knight. Nashville, TN: Nelson, 1984.

Hasel, Gerhard F. "Proposals for a Canonical Biblical Theology." *Andrews University Seminary Studies* 34.1. 1996: 23-33.

Hasel, Gerhard. *Old Testament Theology: Basic Issues in the Current Debate*, 4th ed., Revised and Expanded. Grand Rapids: Eerdmans, 1991.

Hassel, Gerhard. *The Remnant*. Berrien Springs, MI: Andrews University, 1972.

Hengstenberg, E. W. *Christology of the Old Testament*. Grand Rapids: Kregel, 1956.

Josephus' *Antiquities of the Jews*. XI.8:3.

Kaiser, Walter C. Jr. "Name" in *Zondervan Pictorial Encyclopedia of the Bible*, ed. M. C. Tenney. Grand Rapids: Zondervan, 1975: 4:360-70.

Kaiser, Walter C. *The Promise-Plan of God*. Grand Rapids: Zondervan, 2008.

Kaiser, Walter C. Jr. "The Prophetic Use of the Old Testament in the New," in *The Uses of the Old Testament* in the New. Chicago: Moody Press, 1985.

Kaiser, Walter C. Jr. "The Davidic Promise and the Inclusion of the Gentiles (Amos 9:11-15 and Acts 15:13-18): A Test Passage for Theological Systems." *JETS* 20 (1977): 97-111.

Kaiser, Walter C. Jr. "The Unfailing Kindnesses Promised to David: Isaiah 55:3." *JSOT* 45, 1989: 91-98.

Kaiser, Walter C. Jr. *Messiah in the Old Testament*. Grand Rapids: Zondervan, 1995.

Kaiser, Walter C. Jr. *Recovering the Unity of the Bible: One Continuous Story, Plan and Purpose*. Grand Rapids: Zondervan, 2009.

Kaiser, Walter C. Jr., "Massa', in *Theological Wordbook of the Old Testament*, eds. R. Laird Harris, Gleason L Archer, Jr., and Bruce K. Waltke. Chicago: Moody, 1980.

Kaiser, Walter C., Jr. "The Blessing of David: The Charter for Humanity," in *The Law and the Prophets: Old Testament Studies in Honor of O.T. Allis*, ed. John H. Skilton. Phillipsburg, NJ: Presbyterian and Reformed, 1974.

Kaiser, Walter. "Psalm 72: An Historical and Messianic Current Example of Antiochene Hermeneutical *Theoria*," *JETS* 52/2. June 2009.

Kay, W. "Isaiah: Introduction, Commentary and Critical Notes" in *The Bible Commentary*, ed. F. C. Cook, vol 5. Grand Rapids: Baker, 1981.

Keil, C. F. *Biblical Commentary on the Old Testament: Minor Prophets*. Grand Rapids: Eerdmans, 1954.

Kidner, Derek. "Isaiah" in *The New Bible Commentary: 21st Century Edition*, ed., D. A. Carson Grand Rapids: Eerdmans, 1984.

Leupold, H. C. *Exposition of Psalms*. Grand Rapids: Baker, 1974.

MacRae, Allan A. *The Gospel of Isaiah*. Chicago: Moody Press, 1977.

Maier, Gerhard. *Biblical Hermeneutics*, trans. R. W. Yarbrough. Wheaton, IL: Crossway, 1994.

Martens, Elmer. "Tackling Old Testament Theology," *JETS* 20. 1977.

Nassif, Bradley, "*Antiochene Theoria in John Chrysostom's Exegesis*," PhD dissertation, Fordham University, New York, 1991.

Payne, J. Barton. *Encyclopedia of Biblical Prophecy*. New York: Harper and Row, 1973.

Payne, J. Barton. *Encyclopedia of Biblical Prophecy*. Grand Rapids: Baker, 1974.

Robertson, O. Palmer. *The Flow of the Psalms: Discovering their Structure and Theology*. Phillipsburg, NJ: P & R, 2015.

Rowler, H. H. *The Unity of the Bible*. Philadelphia: Westminster Press, 1953.

Saucy, Mark R. "Israel as a Necessary Theme in Biblical Theology," in *The People, The Land, and the Future of Israel: Israel and the Jewish People in the Plan of God*. ed. Darrell L. Bock and Mitch Glaser. Grand Rapids: Kregel, 2014.

Seitz, Christopher. "Royal Promises in the Canonical Books of Isaiah and Psalms," in "Isaiah in Scripture and the Church" (unpublished manuscript, 1994).

Smith, James E. *What the Bible Teaches About the Promised Messiah*. Nashville, TN: Thomas Nelson, 1993.

The Moody Handbook of Messianic Prophecy. Chicago: Moody Publishers, 2019.

Wilson, G. H. "The Use of Royal Psalms at the 'Seams' of the Hebrew Psalter," *JSOT* 35, 1986: 85-94.

www.ingramcontent.com/pod-product-compliance
Lightning Source LLC
LaVergne TN
LVHW010620100826
845148LV00014B/3049